a year with

Six Sisters' STUFF

s   Roast Beef,
    Mashed Potatoes

m   Chicken Pot Pie

t   Soup, Rolls

w   Spaghetti, Salad

t   Leftovers

f   Pizza, Br

s   Mea
       Beans

a year with Six Sisters' STUFF

52 MENU PLANS, RECIPES, AND IDEAS
TO BRING FAMILIES TOGETHER

SHADOW
MOUNTAIN

TO OUR PARENTS, HUSBANDS, AND CHILDREN

FOR ALWAYS LOVING AND SUPPORTING US

(AND FOR ALLOWING US TO PHOTOGRAPH YOUR

DINNER BEFORE YOU COULD EAT IT)

All photographs courtesy SixSistersStuff.com.

Except for the following photographs: page 161 © Wiktory/Shutterstock.com; page 182 © Yeko Photo Studio/Shutterstock.com; page 183 © mikeledray/Shutterstock.com, © Joe Gough/Shutterstock.com, © RoJo Images/Shutterstock.com; and page 210 © wavebreakmedia/Shutterstock.com.

Library of Congress Cataloging-in-Publication Data

A year with Six Sisters' stuff: 52 menu plans, recipes, and ideas to bring families together.
    pages cm
Includes index.
Summary: Compilation of 52 weekly menu plans to help make dinnertime fun and easy for families.
ISBN 978-1-60907-816-4 (paperbound)
1. Cooking. I. Six Sisters.
TX714.Y43 2014
641.5—dc23   2013036834

Printed in China
Global Interprint, Inc., Shenzhen, China

10 9 8 7 6 5 4 3 2

CONTENTS

MENU 1

Slow Cooker Sticky Chicken
Baked Sweet Potato Fries
Strawberry Lemonade Slush

Baked Sweet Potato Fries

I always order sweet potato fries when we go out to dinner. I decided I would attempt to make them at home but didn't want to fry them. That is when this little recipe was born. They were crispy on the outside and soft on the inside, making them absolutely delicious! —Elyse

3 to 4 medium sweet potatoes	½ teaspoon black pepper
3 tablespoons olive oil	½ teaspoon garlic salt
½ teaspoon salt	1 tablespoon cornstarch

Preheat oven to 450 degrees F. Line a large baking sheet with foil and set aside. Wash and peel sweet potatoes. Cut sweet potatoes into fry-shaped slices. Put sweet potatoes in a large, resealable plastic bag and add all other ingredients to the bag. Close the bag and shake until all of the sweet potatoes are evenly coated. Pour contents of the bag onto prepared baking sheet and spread out fries evenly. Bake 40 to 45 minutes, or until browned on the outside, turning fries halfway through.

Makes 6 to 8 servings.

Slow Cooker Sticky Chicken

I love using my slow cooker to simplify dinnertime, and this sweet, sticky sauce is delicious. —Camille

½ cup honey

½ cup light brown sugar

⅓ cup balsamic vinegar

⅓ cup soy sauce

3 garlic cloves, minced

1 teaspoon ground ginger

1 teaspoon Sriracha sauce (or your favorite hot sauce)

Black pepper, to taste

4 to 6 boneless, skinless chicken breasts or thighs

1 tablespoon cornstarch

1 tablespoon water

Fresh cilantro, for garnishing

Sesame seeds, for garnishing

In a medium saucepan, combine honey, brown sugar, balsamic vinegar, soy sauce, garlic, ginger, Sriracha sauce, and black pepper, to taste. Bring sauce to a boil. Reduce heat and simmer 5 minutes, until sugar dissolves and sauce begins to thicken. Remove from heat and cool for a few minutes.

Spray the slow cooker with nonstick cooking spray and place the chicken inside. Pour sauce over chicken and stir to coat chicken. Cover and cook on high 4 hours or on low 6 to 8 hours until chicken registers internal temperature of 165 degrees F. on meat thermometer.

When finished, remove chicken and place on a plate. In a small bowl, mix together cornstarch and water, and pour into the slow cooker with leftover sauce. Mix together well, place chicken back into the slow cooker, and let cook about 10 minutes on high heat, or until the sauce starts to thicken up. Just before serving, sprinkle with torn cilantro leaves and sesame seeds.

Makes 4 to 6 servings.

Strawberry Lemonade Slush

This slush has helped us endure some hot summers! Beat the heat with the sweet flavors of this fruity beverage.

¾ **cup water**

¾ **cup lemonade concentrate, thawed**

1 **(10-ounce) package frozen sweetened strawberries, thawed**

¾ **cup ice cubes**

1 **cup lemon-lime soda**

In a blender, combine water, lemonade concentrate, strawberries, and ice. Blend until fully incorporated.

Pour mixture into a freezer container and freeze for at least 12 hours. (It can be stored in the freezer up to 3 months.)

When ready to serve, remove from freezer and let stand at room temperature about 1 hour before serving.

Divide frozen slush into 4 large glasses and pour ¼ cup lemon-lime soda in each cup. Serve immediately.

Makes 4 servings, but can easily be doubled.

Aloha Burgers
Restaurant-Style Onion Rings
No-Bake Reese's Fudge Bars

Aloha Burgers

To break in my husband's new grill, we tried this recipe. It was amazing, and so easy, too. —Elyse

1⅓ pounds ground beef	4 hamburger buns with sesame seeds
2 cups teriyaki sauce, divided	4 tablespoons mayonnaise
4 pineapple rings	1 tomato, sliced
4 slices cheddar cheese	1 cup shredded lettuce

Form ground beef into 4 equal-sized patties. Pour 1 cup teriyaki sauce over hamburger patties and marinate at least 30 minutes. Pour remaining cup teriyaki sauce into a bowl and let pineapple rings marinate at least 30 minutes. Grill patties over high heat about 3 minutes on each side for medium doneness, longer for well-done burgers. Burgers should reach an internal temperature of 160 degrees F. Place 1 slice cheese on each burger and let the cheese melt before removing burgers from grill. Grill pineapple rings over medium heat for 1 minute on each side.

To assemble burgers, spread ½ tablespoon mayonnaise on both halves of hamburger buns. Place 1 tomato slice on the bottom half of each bun and top with hamburger patty, pineapple ring, shredded lettuce, and remaining bun. Serve with extra teriyaki sauce on the side.

Makes 4 burgers.

Restaurant-Style Onion Rings

Whenever my husband and I go out to eat, I always order onion rings. I would pick onion rings over fries any day of the week! I never thought we would be able to achieve restaurant-quality onion rings at home, but we totally did with this recipe. —Elyse

1   quart vegetable oil

1   large Vidalia onion, cut into ¼-inch slices

1½ cups all-purpose flour

1   teaspoon baking powder

1   teaspoon salt

2   eggs

1   cup milk

1   cup dry bread crumbs

Seasoned salt, to taste

Heat vegetable oil in a deep-fryer or large pot to 365 degrees F. Separate the onion slices into rings and set aside. In a large, shallow bowl, combine flour, baking powder, and salt. Dip the onion slices in the flour mixture until completely coated and set aside. Whisk the eggs and milk into the flour mixture. Dip the floured rings into the batter to coat and place on a wire rack to let excess batter drip off. Pour the bread crumbs into a large bowl. Gently toss battered onions in the bread crumbs to coat evenly. Deep fry a few rings at a time for 2 to 3 minutes, or until golden brown. Place finished onion rings on paper towels to drain. Season with seasoned salt and serve.

Makes 3 to 4 servings.

No-Bake Reese's Fudge Bars

These bars are the perfect combination of fudge and Reese's Peanut Butter Cups.

22 individual Reese's Peanut Butter Cups (regular size), unwrapped and divided

3 cups milk chocolate chips

1 (14-ounce) can sweetened condensed milk

Line a 9x9-inch pan with foil and coat with cooking spray. Place 16 peanut butter cups in an even layer on the bottom of the pan.

Place chocolate chips and sweetened condensed milk in a medium saucepan over low heat. Stir until chips and milk melt together.

Once everything is melted, spread evenly over peanut butter cups in prepared pan. Crumble remaining Reese's Peanut Butter Cups and sprinkle over the top, pressing them lightly into the fudge. Cool on countertop until fudge reaches room temperature, then cover with plastic wrap and place in the refrigerator to harden completely. Cut into squares and serve.

Makes 32 bite-sized servings.

MENU 3

Creamy Chicken Lasagna

Cheesy Garlic Texas Toast

Caesar Salad Supreme

Creamy Chicken Lasagna

When I have a particularly crazy week at home, it's nice to make something warm and filling—and easy!
—Stephanie

- 6 uncooked lasagna noodles
- 3 cups cooked, shredded chicken
- 1 cube chicken bouillon, dissolved in ¼ cup hot water
- 1 (8-ounce) package cream cheese, softened
- 2 cups shredded mozzarella cheese, divided
- 1 (26-ounce) jar spaghetti sauce
  Italian seasoning, to taste

Preheat oven to 350 degrees F. Cook lasagna noodles according to package directions; drain, rinse in cold water, and set aside. In a large bowl, combine shredded chicken, bouillon water, cream cheese, and 1 cup mozzarella. Spread ⅓ of spaghetti sauce in the bottom of a 9x13-inch baking dish. Cover with ½ of the chicken mixture and top with 3 lasagna noodles. Repeat layers. Top with remaining sauce and mozzarella. Sprinkle on Italian seasoning, to taste. Bake 45 minutes, until cheese is melted and bubbly.

Makes 6 to 8 servings.

Cheesy Garlic Texas Toast

I love when my mom makes pasta for dinner because I know she will make garlic bread with it. This is my favorite garlic bread recipe. —Kendra

½ cup unsalted butter, softened

1 teaspoon garlic powder

Salt and pepper, to taste

1 loaf French bread or other white bread, cut into eight 1-inch slices

1 cup shredded mozzarella cheese

Italian seasoning, to taste

Preheat broiler. Mix together butter and garlic powder in a small bowl. Add salt and pepper, to taste. Spread 1½ teaspoons butter mixture on each side of each bread slice; place buttered bread slices on an ungreased baking sheet. Broil bread 1 minute on each side, or until light golden brown. Sprinkle 1 side of bread with cheese and Italian seasoning and broil again until cheese is melted. Watch closely to avoid burning.

Makes 8 servings.

Caesar Salad Supreme

This homemade Caesar salad is perfect for bringing to parties or potlucks. You can prepare the salad earlier in the day and toss in the dressing just before serving.

3 cloves garlic, minced

¾ cup mayonnaise

6 tablespoons grated Parmesan cheese, divided

1 teaspoon Worcestershire sauce

1 teaspoon Dijon mustard

1 tablespoon lemon juice

¼ cup olive oil

Salt, to taste

Freshly ground black pepper, to taste

1 head romaine lettuce, torn into bite-sized pieces

4 cups croutons

In a small bowl, combine garlic, mayonnaise, 2 tablespoons Parmesan cheese, Worcestershire sauce, mustard, lemon juice, and olive oil. Season with salt and black pepper, to taste. Refrigerate until ready to use. Place lettuce in a large bowl. Toss with dressing, remaining Parmesan cheese, and croutons.

Makes 6 servings.

MENU 4

Slow Cooker BBQ Ranch Ribs

Slow Cooker Baked Beans

Cheesy Ranch Potatoes

Slow Cooker BBQ Ranch Ribs

I love using my slow cooker on days when I know I won't have much time to prepare dinner in the evening. This is a simple recipe you can put in your slow cooker in the morning and have an amazing meal by dinnertime. —Elyse

2 pounds boneless country ribs	1½ tablespoons lemon juice
1 (.25-ounce) packet ranch dressing mix	1 tablespoon honey
1½ cups ketchup	2 tablespoons light brown sugar
3 tablespoons yellow mustard	1 teaspoon black pepper
4 tablespoons Worcestershire sauce	Pinch salt
2 tablespoons white vinegar	

Place ribs into slow cooker and sprinkle ranch dressing packet on top. In a medium bowl, whisk together ketchup, mustard, Worcestershire sauce, white vinegar, lemon juice, honey, brown sugar, pepper, and salt. Pour sauce over ribs. Place lid on slow cooker and cook on high 3 to 4 hours or on low 6 to 8 hours. Ribs should measure an internal temperature of 145 degrees F.

Makes 6 servings.

Slow Cooker Baked Beans

These beans taste amazing. They make the house smell so good as they cook in the slow cooker. Perfect as a side dish for almost any meal.

3 (28-ounce) cans pork and beans

1 small onion, diced

1 cup barbecue sauce

¾ cup light brown sugar

2 tablespoons yellow mustard

½ pound bacon, cooked and crumbled

Mix all ingredients, except bacon, in slow cooker. Stir until combined. Cover and cook on low 3 to 5 hours. Crumble cooked bacon on top of beans before serving.

Makes 8 servings.

Cheesy Ranch Potatoes

These ranch potatoes are one of our favorite side dishes. We often triple the recipe when we have the whole family together and there are never any leftovers.

4 large baking potatoes

4 ounces cream cheese, softened

¼ cup sour cream

¼ cup finely chopped yellow onion

1 cup shredded Colby Jack cheese, divided

5 slices cooked bacon, broken into pieces, divided

¼ teaspoon salt

½ cup milk

1 (1-ounce) package dry ranch dressing mix

4 green onions, finely chopped

Wash potatoes and pierce in several places with a fork. Microwave on high 10 minutes until tender. Set aside to cool slightly.

Preheat oven to 350 degrees F. Grease an 11x7-inch baking pan.

Combine cream cheese and sour cream in a large bowl; beat until smooth. Add yellow onion, ½ cup cheese, half of the bacon bits, and salt. Mix well.

When potatoes are cool enough to handle, cut in half. Peel and mash potatoes. Add mashed potatoes to the cream cheese mixture. Beat with a mixer. Stir in milk. Add dry ranch dressing mix and mix in well.

Spread potato mixture in prepared pan. Bake uncovered 30 minutes. Remove from oven, sprinkle with remaining cheese, bacon pieces, and green onions. Bake 5 minutes longer, or until cheese melts.

Makes 8 servings.

MENU 5

Asian Glazed Salmon

Sesame Green Beans

Fresh Fruit with Fluffy Fruit Dip

Fluffy Fruit Dip

This is my go-to fruit dip recipe. It has only two ingredients, but you would never guess by how delicious it is.
—Kendra

1 **(8-ounce) container whipped cream cheese**	1 **(7-ounce) jar marshmallow creme**

Put both ingredients in a bowl and whip vigorously with a wire whisk until smooth and fluffy. Serve with strawberries, bananas, pineapple—basically any kind of fruit. Enjoy!

Makes 2 cups or 8 servings.

Asian Glazed Salmon

Cooking salmon can be intimidating if you have never done it before. I love using pre-cut, frozen fillets. All you have to do is thaw the fish then follow this recipe. —Kristen

¾ **cup light brown sugar**

⅓ **cup soy sauce**

2 **tablespoons hoisin sauce**

2 **tablespoons grated fresh ginger root**
  Crushed red pepper flakes, to taste

½ **teaspoon minced garlic**

1 **tablespoon lime juice**

4 **(5-ounce) boneless, skinless salmon fillets**

In a medium saucepan, whisk together brown sugar, soy sauce, hoisin sauce, ginger, red pepper flakes, garlic, and lime juice. Bring to a boil over medium heat until sauce thickens, between 5 and 10 minutes. Set aside. Preheat the oven broiler to high. Place salmon in a foil-lined baking dish. Baste with glaze and broil 4 minutes. Remove salmon from the oven, turn over, baste with glaze and return to the oven to broil 4 more minutes. Remove the salmon from the oven and glaze one more time before serving. Internal temperature should be 145 degrees F.

Makes 4 servings.

Sesame Green Beans

Do you ever find yourself in a side-dish rut? Add a little something extra to plain green beans to take them over the top. —Kristen

1½ pounds green beans, washed and trimmed

1 tablespoon vegetable oil

2 teaspoons dark sesame oil

½ teaspoon crushed red pepper flakes

2 tablespoons toasted sesame seeds

Salt

Place beans in a large saucepan or wok. Cover with ½ inch of water and boil for 2 minutes. Transfer beans to a colander and run under cold water. Drain well. Heat a wok or large nonstick frying pan over high heat. Drizzle vegetable oil into pan and rotate pan to spread oil. Add sesame oil and crushed red pepper flakes. Add beans and stir-fry 2 minutes. Sprinkle with sesame seeds and salt, to taste. Toss to coat evenly.

Makes 4 servings.

THE "CRAZY DINNER" TRADITION

One of our favorite family traditions started about twenty years ago and is called "Crazy Dinner."

We were all living at home, and it was Thanksgiving Eve. Mom had been in the kitchen all day, prepping and cooking food for our upcoming feast. Dinnertime was getting closer and, after cooking all day, the last thing my mom wanted to do was cook some more. So our parents loaded us all in the van, and we took off for the grocery store.

We were each given $5 and told that we could buy whatever we wanted for dinner–anything! I remember holding my five-dollar bill so tightly as I walked up and down the aisles looking at all the yummy food. I finally decided on a frozen pizza that looked so delicious (as it would to any ten-year-old kid).

I was nervous that my mom would make me put it back, but she didn't even bat an eye when I added my pizza to the cart. My other sisters had already put their items in the cart: crab dip, chicken nuggets, yogurt, French bread, waffles, chocolate cake—the most random meal of all time!

We purchased our items and piled into the van. We were so excited about our purchases and could not wait to get home and eat dinner. We all gathered in the kitchen and started to prepare our items to contribute to the meal.

Once everything was ready, Mom pulled out her nicest tablecloth, china, and candlesticks, and we ate our Crazy Dinner by candlelight. It was, and still is, one of the most memorable dinners of my life.

After that first year, we made this a yearly tradition for dinner on Thanksgiving Eve. Even after my sisters started moving out, we would all try to come home to participate in Crazy Dinner. —Camille

WHAT YOU'LL NEED

- **A set amount of money for each family member (under $10 is ideal)**
- **A nice tablecloth, fancy dishes, and candlesticks**
- **An adventurous palate and a sense of humor**

Honey-Lime Chicken Enchiladas

Easy Mexican Salsa Rice

Piña Colada Cake

Easy Mexican Salsa Rice

One evening, I wanted to spice up our Mexican dinner. I spotted a box of instant brown rice in the pantry and wondered what would happen if I added some ingredients to it. To my surprise it turned out *amazing* and is now a staple side dish whenever we eat Mexican food! —Camille

2 cups instant brown rice	1 cup salsa
2 cups water	1 (4-ounce) can green chilies
1 (1-ounce) envelope enchilada sauce mix or taco seasoning mix	

Combine all ingredients in a microwave-safe bowl. Heat on high power 8 to 9 minutes, or until rice is tender. Let sit 3 to 5 minutes until rice soaks up most of the liquid in the bowl. Fluff with a fork and serve.

Makes 8 servings.

Honey-Lime Chicken Enchiladas

This is my husband's all-time favorite meal. Whenever I have to take a meal to neighbors, or when people are coming over, my husband always thinks I should make this. I'm sure everyone we know has eaten these by now. —Kristen

6 tablespoons honey	2 cups green enchilada sauce, divided
5 tablespoons lime juice	8 to 10 flour tortillas
1 tablespoon chili powder	4 cups shredded Monterey Jack cheese, divided
½ teaspoon garlic powder	
2 to 3 cups cooked, shredded chicken	1 cup heavy whipping cream

Whisk the first four ingredients and toss with shredded chicken in a resealable plastic bag. Let chicken marinate in the fridge for at least 30 minutes, but preferably half a day or so.

Preheat oven to 350 degrees F. Pour about ½ cup green enchilada sauce on the bottom of a 9x13-inch baking pan. Remove chicken from bag, reserving any leftover marinade, and set aside. Fill the tortillas with chicken and shredded cheese, saving about 1 cup cheese to sprinkle on top of enchiladas. Place rolled tortillas in 9x13-inch pan as you go.

Mix the remaining enchilada sauce with the cream and leftover marinade. Pour sauce on top of the enchiladas. Sprinkle with remaining cheese. Bake 30 minutes, until brown and crispy on top.

Makes 8 to 10 servings.

Piña Colada Cake

Our Grandma Char's cousin Maxine gave us this recipe. It's so moist and delicious! We like to eat it in the wintertime to help us think warm thoughts. If you close your eyes as you chew, you can escape the cold and imagine a warm summer evening.

1   (15.25-ounce) yellow cake mix and ingredients called for on box

1   (15-ounce) can crushed pineapple, drained (reserve liquid)

1   (14-ounce) can sweetened condensed milk

1   cup cream of coconut

2   cups heavy whipping cream

½   cup powdered sugar

1½   cups shredded coconut

Bake cake in a 9x13-inch pan according to directions on the box. When cake is baked and still warm, use the end of a wooden mixing spoon to poke holes all over the top of the cake.

Mix reserved pineapple juice, sweetened condensed milk, and coconut cream in a small bowl. Pour mixture over the top of the cake, making sure to fill each hole. Let the cake cool completely.

In a large bowl, using an electric mixer, whip the cream with the powdered sugar until soft peaks form. Top cake with drained, crushed pineapple. Spread sweetened whipped cream on top and sprinkle with coconut.

Makes 16 servings.

Grilled Pineapple Pork Chops
Slow Cooker Roasted Vegetables
Nutty Caramel Bars

Nutty Caramel Bars

I love it when desserts have only a few ingredients, take a few minutes to make, and taste amazing! These Nutty Caramel Bars fit that description perfectly. These sweet, chocolaty bars are to die for. I usually have to give them all away to stop myself from eating the whole pan. —Camille

2 cups all-purpose flour	½ cup chopped walnuts
1 cup light brown sugar	1 (19-ounce) jar caramel ice cream topping
¾ cup unsalted butter, softened	
½ cup chopped pecans	2 cups milk chocolate chips

Preheat oven to 350 degrees F. In a large bowl, combine flour and brown sugar. Mix in butter until combined and crumbly. Press mixture into an ungreased 9x13-inch baking dish. Sprinkle on pecans and walnuts. Drizzle caramel topping evenly over nuts. Bake 15 to 20 minutes or until caramel is bubbly. Remove from oven and sprinkle on chocolate chips. Let stand for 5 minutes. Carefully spread melted chips over caramel layer. Let cool at room temperature or until chocolate sets. Cut into bars.

Makes 24 bars.

Grilled Pineapple Pork Chops

Sometimes pork chops have a reputation for being dry or lacking flavor; however, this recipe proves exactly the opposite! Who knew that a couple of pantry staples would make one of the best pork chops I have ever had? —Camille

1 (20-ounce) can pineapple rings, juice reserved

½ cup light brown sugar

½ cup soy sauce

½ teaspoon garlic powder

4 to 6 pork chops

Mix together pineapple juice (reserved from the can of pineapple rings), brown sugar, soy sauce, and garlic powder in a large resealable plastic bag until all the sugar is dissolved. Add pork chops and zip closed. Store in the fridge 8 to 12 hours.

When ready to cook, preheat grill to medium-high heat. Remove chops from bag and place on grill. Brush pork chops with marinade while they are cooking to let the flavor soak in.

Grill until pork chops are browned and no longer pink inside (about 6 to 8 minutes per side, depending on thickness of chops). Internal temperature should register 145 degrees F.

While chops are cooking, place pineapple rings on grill and cook until they are warmed through and have slight grill marks on them. Serve pork chops with grilled pineapple on top.

Makes 4 to 6 servings.

Slow Cooker Roasted Vegetables

For this recipe, you can use whatever vegetables you have available. I love making these in the summer because they take hardly any time to prepare, and my kitchen stays cool since I don't need to use my oven. —Camille

4	unpeeled potatoes, scrubbed and chopped into large pieces (any kind of potato will work)
2	carrots, sliced
½	onion, sliced
2	zucchinis, thickly sliced (these cook faster than the other vegetables, so make them pretty thick)

Olive oil

1 (6-ounce) packet dry Italian dressing mix

Freshly grated Parmesan cheese, for garnishing

Place chopped vegetables in a large bowl. Drizzle vegetables with olive oil. Sprinkle packet of dressing mix over the vegetables. Lightly toss so that all the vegetables are covered in oil and seasoning. Spray slow cooker with nonstick cooking spray and pour seasoned vegetables inside. Cook on low 5 to 7 hours or high 3 to 4 hours. Sprinkle with fresh Parmesan cheese and enjoy! Other vegetables we like to use include green peppers, asparagus, yellow zucchini squash, snap peas, and fresh green beans.

Makes 6 servings.

Crispy Onion Chicken

Marinated Italian Salad

Nutella Peanut Butter
Swirl Cookies

Crispy Onion Chicken

With a picky three-year-old, I often find myself making a bowl of Easy Mac to avoid a mealtime meltdown. This recipe, however, is an answer to my picky-eater prayers! To quote my three-year-old, "It is like a big, yummy chicken nugget!" —Elyse

4   boneless, skinless chicken breasts

¾   cup honey mustard

2   cups French's French Fried Onions, crushed

Preheat oven to 375 degrees F. Line a casserole dish with foil and coat with cooking spray. Dip each chicken breast in honey mustard and coat in crushed onions. Place in prepared dish and bake 30 to 35 minutes, or until internal temperature registers 165 degrees F.

Makes 4 servings.

Marinated Italian Salad

This salad is the perfect way to use fresh vegetables. Your vegetables will be full of flavor after soaking in this delicious marinade overnight!

4   cups fresh broccoli florets

3   cups chopped cauliflower

½   pound sliced fresh mushrooms

2   cups sliced cucumbers

1   (16-ounce) bottle Italian salad dressing

1   (6-ounce) envelope dry Italian dressing mix

1   pint cherry tomatoes, halved

1   (2¼-ounce) can sliced ripe olives, drained

Shredded Parmesan cheese, for garnishing

In a large serving bowl, combine broccoli, cauliflower, mushrooms, and cucumber. In a small bowl, combine dressing and dressing mix; drizzle over vegetables and toss to coat. Cover and refrigerate overnight. Just before serving, add tomatoes and olives and toss to coat. Top with shredded Parmesan cheese.

Makes 6 to 8 servings.

Nutella Peanut Butter Swirl Cookies

I have a confession: before trying this recipe I had never eaten Nutella. I just love chocolate so much, I had always thought, "Why waste my time on anything else?" Until I saw this recipe. This cookie dough is so good I was eating it by the spoonful, and the baked cookies were even better. —Stephanie

½   **cup unsalted butter, room temperature**

¾   **cup creamy peanut butter**

½   **cup granulated sugar**

½   **cup packed light brown sugar**

1   **egg**

½   **teaspoon vanilla extract**

1¾   **cups all-purpose flour**

¾   **teaspoon baking soda**

¼   **teaspoon salt**

¼   **cup Nutella**

Preheat oven to 350 degrees F. Using an electric mixer, beat together butter, peanut butter, and sugars until light and fluffy, about 2 to 3 minutes. Add in egg and vanilla and beat until well combined.

In a separate bowl, combine flour, baking soda, and salt. With mixer on low (or by hand), slowly incorporate dry ingredients into the butter mixture until just combined.

Microwave Nutella on high power for 20 seconds and then drizzle over the dough. Fold in Nutella with a spatula until well distributed throughout the dough to give it a marbled look.

Chill dough in the refrigerator 15 minutes and then roll small balls by hand. Place about an inch apart on an ungreased cookie sheet and use a fork to press the balls down slightly. Bake until the edges are lightly browned, about 8 to 10 minutes. Allow cookies to cool on the pan 2 minutes, and then transfer to a cooling rack to cool completely.

Makes 40 cookies.

Honey Baked Ham

Homemade Scalloped Potatoes

Cherry Pie Bars

Homemade Scalloped Potatoes

This recipe has simple ingredients and comes together quickly and easily. If you have a potato lover at your table, be ready to serve up seconds! —Camille

3 tablespoons butter	1½ cups shredded sharp cheddar cheese, divided
3 tablespoons all-purpose flour	
1½ cups milk	4 to 6 russet potatoes, peeled and thinly sliced (about 4 cups)
1 teaspoon salt	
Pinch cayenne pepper	Paprika, to taste

Preheat oven to 350 degrees F. In a small saucepan, melt butter over low heat. Stir in flour until incorporated. Slowly add milk and whisk well. Add salt and cayenne pepper, to taste. Continue to cook sauce on low heat until it boils, stirring often with whisk.

Remove from heat and add 1 cup cheese. Stir well until cheese is melted and sauce is smooth.

Spray a 9x9-inch baking pan with nonstick cooking spray. Layer half of the potatoes and pour half of the cheese sauce over potatoes. Repeat with remaining potatoes and cheese sauce and top with shredded cheese. Sprinkle paprika on top and bake, uncovered, 1 hour.

Makes 6 servings.

Honey Baked Ham

One of my Grandma's best recipes is for her delicious ham. She is just a tiny little thing, but she can cook like nobody's business! This recipe is pretty close to the ham she makes, but I made it a little bit simpler by throwing it in my slow cooker. —Camille

1	(7- to 10-pound) spiral ham	¼	teaspoon ground nutmeg
⅓	cup plus 1 tablespoon water, divided	½	teaspoon ground cinnamon
½	cup light brown sugar	2	tablespoons spicy Dijon mustard
½	cup honey	2	tablespoons cornstarch

Spray slow cooker with nonstick cooking spray. Place ham and ⅓ cup water in the slow cooker.

Combine sugar, honey, nutmeg, cinnamon, and mustard in a saucepan over medium heat. Let cook 2 to 5 minutes, until ingredients melt and combine; whisk thoroughly. Remove from heat and pour honey/brown sugar mixture over the ham. Cover and cook the ham on low 6 to 8 hours. Baste the ham with the juices in the slow cooker once every hour. The ham should reach an internal temperature of 145 degrees F.

Remove cooked ham from the slow cooker and set aside for carving.

Pour the juices from the slow cooker into a medium saucepan. Mix together cornstarch and 1 tablespoon water and pour into the saucepan. Cook over medium heat, whisking frequently, until sauce starts to thicken. Use that as a glaze over the ham or even as a gravy for potatoes.

You can also bake this ham in your oven. Place in deep baking pan and cover (making a tin foil tent if needed) and bake 15 to 20 minutes per pound at 350 degrees F. Baste ham once every thirty minutes.

Makes 14 to 18 servings.

Cherry Pie Bars

The crust for these bars almost tastes like a sugar cookie, and they are dangerously delicious!

1 cup unsalted butter, softened

2 cups granulated sugar

4 eggs

1 teaspoon vanilla extract

¼ teaspoon almond extract

3 cups all-purpose flour

1 teaspoon salt

1 (21-ounce) can cherry pie filling

GLAZE

1 cup powdered sugar

½ teaspoon vanilla extract

½ teaspoon almond extract

2 tablespoons milk

Preheat oven to 350 degrees F. In a large bowl, cream together butter and sugar. Add eggs, vanilla extract, and almond extract and beat well. Add flour and salt to the creamed mixture and mix until combined.

Grease a 9x13-inch baking pan and spread about ¾ of the batter in the bottom. (If dough is a little sticky, spray your hands with nonstick cooking spray and use your hands to spread the dough to the edges of the pan.) Spread pie filling over the batter. Drop remaining batter on top of pie filling in teaspoonful amounts.

Bake 35 minutes or until toothpick inserted through crust comes out clean. Combine glaze ingredients and drizzle over the bars.

Makes 15 servings.

MENU 10

Stuffed Mexican Chicken Shells

Fast Three-Bean Salad

Fudge Crinkle Cookies

Fudge Crinkle Cookies

These cookies are quick and easy to make but taste like you spent a lot of time on them. They are fudgy and chewy—I have yet to meet a person who doesn't like them. The best part about these cookies is that they require only 4 ingredients (and I bet you have them in your pantry right now). —Kendra

1 (18.25-ounce) box devil's food cake mix

½ cup vegetable oil

2 eggs

½ cup powdered sugar (for rolling the cookies in)

Preheat oven to 350 degrees F. Stir together the dry cake mix (do not follow directions on the box—you just want to use the dry mix that is in the box), oil, and eggs in a large bowl until dough forms. Dust hands with powdered sugar and shape dough into 1- to 1½-inch balls. Roll balls in powdered sugar and place 2 inches apart on ungreased cookie sheets. Bake 7 to 9 minutes, until center is just set. Remove from pans after a minute or so and cool on wire racks.

Makes 36 cookies.

Stuffed Mexican Chicken Shells

This is a great freezer meal because it makes so much. Bake 1 pan for dinner the night you make this, and then wrap the other uncooked pan with foil and throw it in the freezer to eat on another night. When you are ready to put it on the menu, let it thaw in the fridge 24 hours, and bake 30 minutes at 350 degrees F.

40 large pasta shells	3 (8-ounce) packages cream cheese, softened (not melted)
4 cups cooked and diced chicken breast	¼ cup chicken broth
1 (15-ounce) can black beans, rinsed and drained	2 (14-ounce) cans diced tomatoes with chilies, undrained (Rotel or store brand)
6 green onions, diced	2 cups salsa, divided
1 green bell pepper, diced	1½ cups shredded sharp cheddar cheese
1 red bell pepper, diced	
1 teaspoon cumin	

Preheat oven to 350 degrees F.

Cook pasta shells in well-salted, boiling water until almost al dente (they need to be firm to make them easier to stuff). Drain the pasta and set aside while preparing the filling.

Mix diced chicken, black beans, green onions, peppers, and cumin in a large bowl. In a separate bowl, mix the cream cheese, chicken broth, and undrained tomatoes. When thoroughly combined, pour cream cheese mixture over the chicken mixture and mix well. (If you have trouble incorporating the cream cheese and tomatoes, you can heat them slightly in the microwave.)

You will need either two 9x13-inch baking pans or one large baking sheet. Spread ¾ cup salsa in the bottom of each 9x13-inch baking pan. Using a spoon, fill each of your cooked pasta shells with chicken mixture, placing them in the salsa-covered pan. Repeat until all shells are filled and arranged in the pans. Drizzle shells with the remaining ½ cup of salsa (¼ cup per pan), then sprinkle with the shredded cheese. Cover pans tightly with foil and bake about 30 minutes, until hot and bubbly.

Makes 12 to 15 servings.

Fast Three-Bean Salad

Like many bean salads, it's even better the next day once the dressing has soaked into the beans and veggies.
—Kristen

1 (15-ounce) can chickpeas	1 cup chopped romaine lettuce
1 (15-ounce) can red kidney beans	⅓ cup finely chopped fresh parsley
1 cup cooked chopped green beans	3 green onions, finely chopped
1 red bell pepper, finely chopped	Salt and pepper, to taste

DRESSING

4 tablespoons fresh lemon juice (about 1½ lemons)	1 tablespoon pure maple syrup
1½ tablespoons extra virgin olive oil, or more to taste	1 tablespoon Dijon mustard
1 tablespoon apple cider vinegar	¼ teaspoon salt

Drain and rinse chickpeas and kidney beans and place them in a large bowl with green beans, red pepper, romaine lettuce, parsley, and green onions. Toss together.

In a small bowl, whisk together dressing ingredients until combined. Adjust to taste if needed.

Pour dressing over salad and mix well. Refrigerate 30 minutes to allow the flavors to develop. Season with salt and pepper and adjust dressing to taste. Store in the fridge 3 to 4 days.

Makes 5 cups.

THE SIX SISTERS' PANTRY STAPLES

We focus on creating recipes with foods that are already in your pantry so you don't have to go out and buy a huge list of ingredients. We are always asked what kinds of foods we have in our own pantries, which is why we put together this list of pantry staples. It may not be the same for everyone, but these are some items that the Six Sisters just can't cook without!

BAKING INGREDIENTS

All-purpose flour

Baking powder

Baking soda

Brown sugar

Cake mix

Chocolate chips

Cooking spray

Granulated sugar

Oats

Peanut butter

Powdered sugar

Sweetened condensed milk

Vanilla extract

SPICES

Basil

Black pepper

Chili powder

Cinnamon

Cumin

Garlic salt

Italian seasoning

Nutmeg

Onion powder

Oregano

Parsley

Sage

Salt

COOKING INGREDIENTS

Beef broth

Bread crumbs

Canned black beans

Canned chili

Canned corn

Canned mandarin oranges

Canned pineapple chunks

Canned tuna

Chicken broth

Cornstarch

Cream of chicken soup

Cream of mushroom soup

Extra virgin olive oil

Honey

Jell-O (a must-have in Utah!)

Noodles

Onion soup mix

Pasta sauce

Ranch dressing packets

Red and green bell peppers

Rice

Salad dressing (We always have Italian dressing on hand)

Salsa

Taco seasoning packets

Tomato paste

Tomato sauce

Vegetable oil

Vinegar

M E N U 11

Slow Cooker Creamy Spaghetti

Cheesy Artichoke Bread

Almond Joy Cookies

Cheesy Artichoke Bread

I love artichoke dip, so when I found this recipe I knew I had to make it. It was so good, and it makes the perfect side dish! —Stephanie

- 1 (14-ounce) can artichoke hearts, drained and chopped
- 2 green onions, sliced
- 2 cloves garlic, chopped
- 1 (4-ounce) package cream cheese, room temperature
- ¼ cup mayonnaise
- ½ cup sour cream
- ½ cup grated mozzarella, divided
- ¼ cup grated Parmigiano-Reggiano, divided
- 1 loaf Italian bread, sliced in half lengthwise

Preheat oven to 350 degrees F. Mix artichoke hearts, green onions, garlic, cream cheese, mayonnaise, sour cream, mozzarella, and Parmigiano-Reggiano, reserving some of the cheeses.

Create a hollow by removing a half-inch layer of bread from each half of the loaf. Spread mixture into the hollows in the loaf halves and top with reserved cheese. Cover with foil and bake 20 minutes.

Remove the foil and continue to bake until the cheese is melted and golden brown.

Make 6 servings.

Slow Cooker Creamy Spaghetti

Spaghetti is one meal my whole family will eat. Between my love of spaghetti and my obsession for my slow cooker, this is the perfect dinner. The best part? Most of these ingredients are probably already in your kitchen cabinets. —Camille

1 pound Italian sausage

½ teaspoon salt

½ teaspoon black pepper

½ teaspoon garlic salt

3 (24-ounce) jars of pasta sauce, divided

1 pound spaghetti noodles

½ cup Parmesan cheese (grated or powder)

4 ounces fat-free cream cheese

1 (14.5-ounce) can chicken broth

Brown Italian sausage in a medium skillet on stove top until completely cooked through. Season sausage with salt, pepper, and garlic salt. Drain excess grease and set aside.

Pour 1 jar of pasta sauce into slow cooker. Break all spaghetti noodles in half and place on top of sauce. Pour browned sausage over noodles and sprinkle on Parmesan cheese.

Cut cream cheese into bite-sized pieces and place on top of Parmesan. Pour another jar of pasta sauce over cream cheese.

Cover slow cooker with lid and cook on high 3 hours. After 3 hours, remove lid and stir contents. Pour in the last jar of pasta sauce and can of chicken broth. Replace lid and cook another hour on low, or until ready to serve.

Makes 10 to 12 servings.

Almond Joy Cookies

Almond Joys are one of my favorite candy bars. I didn't believe there was anything that even compared until my mom made these cookies. They are *delicious* and taste just like an Almond Joy candy bar. —Kristen

COOKIE

2 (7-ounce) packages sweetened, shredded coconut

1 (14-ounce) can sweetened condensed milk

2 tablespoons sour cream

1 tablespoon heavy whipping cream

1½ teaspoons vanilla extract

TOPPING

1 package milk chocolate or semisweet chocolate chips

2 teaspoons vegetable oil

24 whole almonds

Preheat oven to 325 degrees F. Line baking sheet with parchment paper. In a large bowl, mix all ingredients for the cookie together. Spoon out dough with a small ice cream scoop or spoon and place on cookie sheet. Bake 17 to 18 minutes. Remove from oven and cool.

In a small bowl, make the topping by microwaving chocolate chips and oil about 1 minute. Stir until melted. Spoon chocolate over cookies and top with a whole almond.

Makes 24 cookies.

MENU 12

Pork Chop and Hash Brown Casserole

Nut and Berry Salad

Triple Chocolate Bundt Cake

Triple Chocolate Bundt Cake

This cake could also be called Death by Chocolate—it's dangerously rich and delicious! Grab a large glass of milk and dig in because it's worth every calorie.

- 1 (18.25-ounce) package devil's food chocolate cake mix
- 1 (3.9-ounce) box instant chocolate pudding mix
- 1 cup sour cream
- 1 cup vegetable oil

- 4 eggs
- ½ cup warm water
- 1 cup milk chocolate chips

  Powdered sugar or frosting, for garnishing (optional)

Preheat oven to 350 degrees F. Spray Bundt pan with cooking spray. In a large bowl, mix together cake and pudding mixes, sour cream, oil, eggs, and water. Stir in chocolate chips and pour batter into pan.

Bake 45 to 50 minutes, or until top is springy to the touch and a wooden toothpick inserted comes out clean. Cool cake thoroughly in pan for about 90 minutes before inverting onto a plate. Dust the cake with powdered sugar or frost with your favorite frosting and serve alongside your favorite ice cream.

Makes 10 servings.

Pork Chop and Hash Brown Casserole

This recipe is a side and main dish in one. Doesn't get much better than that!

4 to 6 boneless pork chops

1 tablespoon vegetable oil

   Seasoned salt, to taste

1 (10.5-ounce) can condensed cream of celery soup

½ cup milk

½ cup sour cream

¼ teaspoon black pepper

4 tablespoons butter, melted

½ teaspoon garlic powder

1 (32-ounce) bag frozen hash browns

1 cup shredded cheddar cheese, divided

1 (6-ounce) container French fried onions, divided

Preheat oven to 350 degrees F. Brown pork chops in vegetable oil in pan over medium heat. Sprinkle pork chops with seasoned salt and set aside. In a large mixing bowl, combine soup, milk, sour cream, pepper, melted butter, garlic powder, frozen hash browns, ½ cup shredded cheese, and half the container of French fried onions. Spoon mixture into a 9x13-inch dish and place pork chops on top.

Cover and bake 40 minutes. Remove from oven and top with remaining cheese and onions and bake uncovered 5 additional minutes.

Makes 6 servings.

Nut and Berry Salad

The sweetness of the berries pairs with the tartness in the dressing to make the perfect salad!

½ cup Heinz Gourmet Salad Vinegar

1 teaspoon dry mustard

1 (¾-inch) slice purple onion, finely minced

½ teaspoon salt

1 tablespoon poppy seeds

¾ cup granulated sugar

1 cup vegetable oil

1 bag mixed greens salad

1 bag baby spinach

Feta cheese, for garnishing

Sliced strawberries, for garnishing

Blueberries, for garnishing

Glazed walnuts, for garnishing

Place all ingredients except salad, spinach, Feta, berries, and nuts in a blender or food processor. Blend well. Toss salad and spinach together in a large bowl. Pour dressing over salad. Top with cheese, strawberries, blueberries, and glazed walnuts.

Makes 4 to 6 servings.

Korean Beef and Rice

Ambrosia Fruit Salad

Baked Apple Pie Egg Rolls

Ambrosia Fruit Salad

Before I got married, my grandma gave me the following recipe for this simple ambrosia salad. I still have the recipe card with her teeny-tiny perfect handwriting, and it will forever be a treasure to me. And she is exactly right—it doesn't get much simpler than this little recipe. —Camille

1 (14-ounce) can fruit cocktail	**Other fruit you can add:**
1 (20-ounce) can pineapple tidbits	1 cup green grapes
2 (6-ounce) containers vanilla yogurt	1 cup red grapes
½ cup shredded sweetened coconut	1 apple, diced
1 cup miniature marshmallows	1 banana, sliced
	1 can mandarin oranges

Mix all ingredients together in a large bowl. Chill until served. Prepare no more than 30 minutes before serving, or marshmallows will get mushy.

Makes 8 to 10 servings.

Korean Beef and Rice

I love making dinner in my slow cooker, but what happens when you forget to throw those ingredients in the slow cooker and 5 P.M. rolls around and your kids are whining because they are hungry and you are tired after a long day?

That's when I make Korean Beef and Rice. It's delicious and can be thrown together in one episode of Mickey Mouse Clubhouse! —Camille

1 tablespoon sesame oil	¼ teaspoon ground ginger
1 pound lean ground beef	Salt and pepper, to taste
3 cloves garlic, minced	½ to 1 teaspoon crushed red pepper flakes (depending on how spicy you like it)
½ cup light brown sugar	2 to 3 cups cooked white rice
¼ cup soy sauce	1 bunch green onions, diced

Heat sesame oil in a large skillet over medium heat until shimmering. And ground beef and minced garlic and brown until no more pink remains. Drain off most of the fat and add brown sugar, soy sauce, ginger, salt, pepper, and crushed red pepper. Simmer for a few minutes to blend the flavors. Serve over steamed rice and top with green onions.

Makes 6 servings.

Baked Apple Pie Egg Rolls

We love apple pie, but this is a great alternative when you are short on time. Classic apple pie filling is wrapped up and baked in wonton wrappers for a quick and delicious treat! All the goodness of apple pie in a yummy, hand-held snack!

- 2 whole apples, peeled and diced (Granny Smith works well)
- 3 tablespoons lemon juice
- 1/3 cup granulated sugar
- 4 tablespoons all-purpose flour
- 2 teaspoons ground cinnamon
- 1/4 teaspoon ground allspice
- 1/8 teaspoon salt
- 1 egg, beaten
- 10 egg roll wrappers
- 1 tablespoon butter, melted
- 2 teaspoons cinnamon-sugar mix

Preheat oven to 375 degrees F. Line a large baking sheet with parchment paper and lightly spray the parchment with nonstick cooking spray. In a bowl, stir together apples, lemon juice, and sugar. Add the flour, spices, and salt.

Beat the egg in a separate small bowl. Lay out one egg roll wrapper at a time, brushing the edge with the egg. Scoop about 2 tablespoons apple filling toward one edge of the wrapper, leaving a small border. Fold in the sides and roll up the egg roll tightly. Place it on the baking sheet. Repeat until all the filling has been used.

Bake 20 minutes. Remove from oven and brush each egg roll with melted butter and sprinkle with cinnamon sugar. Return to the oven 5 more minutes.

Serve topped with whipped cream.

Makes 10 egg rolls.

MENU 14

Blackened Salmon Tacos

Perfect Pineapple Dip with Crackers

Banana Cookies

Perfect Pineapple Dip

I love snacks! Sometimes I just need something different than a cheese stick or yogurt. This is an easy dip to prepare and tastes amazing. —Kendra

8	ounces fat-free cream cheese, softened	4	green onions, chopped
¾	can crushed pineapple, drained		Pinch salt

Mix all ingredients together. Spread on crackers (Wheat Thins, Ritz, or Triscuits are recommended). Makes 6 servings.

Blackened Salmon Tacos

Tacos and salmon are two of my most favorite things. Once you taste them paired in this recipe, along with the avocado salsa, you will never go back to regular tacos! —Kristen

BLACKENED SALMON

- 2 tablespoons canola oil
- 2 tablespoons flour
- 2 teaspoons chili powder
- 2 teaspoons brown sugar
- ½ teaspoon onion powder
- ½ teaspoon garlic powder
- ½ teaspoon cumin
- ½ teaspoon salt
- ½ teaspoon black pepper
- 1 pound salmon
  Salt and pepper, to taste

AVOCADO SALSA

- 1 ripe avocado, finely chopped
- 1 large ear of corn, kernels cut off
- 1 tomato, seeds removed and diced
- ¼ cup red onion, diced
- 2 tablespoons cilantro, chopped
- 1 lime, juiced, divided
  Salt and pepper, to taste

CILANTRO RANCH DRESSING

- ¼ cup Greek yogurt
- 2 tablespoons mayonnaise
- 2 tablespoons buttermilk
- 1 small clove garlic
- 2 tablespoons green onions, thinly sliced
- ¼ cup cilantro leaves
  Salt and pepper, to taste

Heat oil in a skillet over medium-high heat. In a small bowl, stir together flour, chili powder, brown sugar, onion powder, garlic powder, cumin, salt, and pepper.

Coat salmon with the blackening spice. Place salmon in hot skillet. Cook about 5 minutes per side, or until coating is blackened and forms a nice crust and salmon is cooked through. (Internal temperature should measure 145 degrees F.) Flake fish with fork. Set aside.

Make the salsa by mixing avocado, corn, tomato, red onion, cilantro, half of the lime juice, salt, and pepper in a large bowl. Refrigerate until ready to serve.

In a food processor, add yogurt, mayonnaise, buttermilk, remaining lime juice, garlic, green onions, cilantro, salt, and pepper. Blend until smooth. Add more buttermilk as needed until desired consistency is reached. (You'll want it to be thin enough to drizzle, but not so thin that it slides off the tacos.) Refrigerate until ready to serve.

To assemble the tacos, place salmon in the center of a warm tortilla. Top with salsa and drizzle with dressing.

Makes 8 servings.

Banana Cookies

Use those overripe bananas on your counter to make these moist, sweet banana cookies. —Kendra

1 cup granulated sugar

½ cup unsalted butter, softened

½ cup shortening

1 teaspoon vanilla extract

2 eggs

3 ripe, mashed bananas (about 1 cup)

½ cup buttermilk

1½ teaspoons baking soda

½ teaspoon salt

3¼ cups all-purpose flour

1 recipe Banana Frosting

Preheat oven to 350 degrees F. In a large bowl, cream together sugar, butter, shortening, and vanilla until light and fluffy. Mix in eggs and bananas. Blend in buttermilk. Add the dry ingredients until just combined. Do not over-beat. It will be a sticky batter. Drop by tablespoons onto a greased cookie sheet. Bake 9 to 10 minutes, until slightly golden. Cool completely on wire racks.

Makes 36 cookies.

Spread Banana Frosting over cooled cookies and serve.

BANANA FROSTING

2 tablespoons unsalted butter, melted

1 to 2 ripe bananas, mashed (depending on how much banana flavor you want)

3 to 4 cups powdered sugar (more or less, depending on the consistency you like)

2 tablespoons milk

1 teaspoon vanilla extract

Mix all ingredients together and spread over cooled cookies.

PERSONALIZED PLATES

When we were small, all six girls had a specific place to sit at the dinner table. Now that I have a family of my own, my girls do the same thing. They have their own spot and like their special seat. I decided I wanted to make their seat even more special by having their very own personalized plate. I let my kids decorate their own and they loved it.

My girls were so excited to have a plate of their very own! This activity would be a fun gift for Grandma, Grandpa, or even Dad! —Kristen

WHAT YOU'LL NEED

- White, oven-safe dinnerware (I chose dessert plates, but you could use mugs or bowls)
- Sharpie marker(s) in a variety of colors
- Glass cleaner
- Oven

INSTRUCTIONS

1. **Clean your plate thoroughly with glass cleaner. Make sure the sticker on the back of the plate is removed.**

2. **Invite your kids** to color, decorate, or design the plate.

3. **After the kids are done coloring,** place the plates directly on the cold oven racks. Heat the oven to 350 degrees F. and set the timer for 30 minutes.

4. **When the plates are done cooking,** take them out and let them cool.

Note: Washing the plates in the dishwasher will cause some colors to fade. Washing the plates by hand will help keep the original colors.

Slow Cooker Eight-Can Taco Soup

Homemade Breadsticks

Fudgy Brownies

Slow Cooker Eight-Can Taco Soup

I keep these ingredients stocked in my pantry for those crazy nights when I need a fast meal. If you don't have a slow cooker, you can easily prepare this in a large stockpot over medium heat for about 20 minutes. —Camille

1 (15-ounce) can black beans, drained and rinsed

1 (15-ounce) can pinto beans, drained and rinsed

1 (14.5-ounce) can diced tomatoes, drained

1 (15-ounce) can sweet corn, drained

1 (12.5-ounce) can chicken breast, drained

1 (10.75-ounce) can condensed cream of chicken soup

1 (10-ounce) can green enchilada sauce

1 (14-ounce) can chicken broth

1 (1-ounce) packet taco seasoning

Spray slow cooker with nonstick cooking spray. Pour all the ingredients into slow cooker and stir together. Cook on low heat 2 to 3 hours. Top with shredded cheese and serve with tortilla chips.

Makes 8 servings.

Homemade Breadsticks

One thing I love about breadsticks is that they go perfect with any soup. These particular ones are so easy and taste delicious. —Elyse

1½ cups warm water

2 tablespoons granulated sugar

1 tablespoon instant yeast

3½ cups all-purpose flour

1 teaspoon salt

3 tablespoons butter, melted

1 teaspoon garlic salt

Kosher salt, to taste

Grated Parmesan cheese, for garnishing

Preheat oven to 400 degrees F. Combine water, sugar, and yeast in a large bowl. Let sit 5 minutes. Stir in flour and salt and mix until smooth. Let dough rise, uncovered, for 10 minutes.

Roll out dough into a large square on a floured surface. Combine butter and garlic and brush over dough. Sprinkle with kosher salt. Fold dough in half and cut into 1-inch strips. Twist each strip and place on a greased baking sheet. Cover and let rise 15 to 20 minutes. Bake 20 minutes or until golden brown. Immediately after baking, brush with more garlic butter and sprinkle with kosher salt and grated Parmesan cheese.

Serve with marinara or alfredo sauce, or ranch dressing for dipping.

*This dough also makes a great pizza dough—just roll out into a large circle, add your favorite toppings, and bake 15 to 20 minutes at 400 degrees F.

Makes 6 servings.

Fudgy Brownies

Our maternal grandma passed away when Mom was a teenager. We never met her, but she was known for these amazing, fudgy brownies. She must have passed on her love for chocolate to all of us!

BROWNIES

1 cup margarine, melted	1 teaspoon vanilla extract
8 tablespoons cocoa powder	2½ cups all-purpose flour
2 cups granulated sugar	1 cup chopped walnuts (optional)
4 eggs	Pinch salt

FROSTING

4 cups powdered sugar	¼ cup hot water
¼ cup margarine, softened	1 teaspoon vanilla extract
3 tablespoons cocoa powder	

Preheat oven to 325 degrees F. Grease a 9x13-inch baking pan; set aside. Combine melted margarine and cocoa powder and set aside. Combine sugar and eggs in a separate mixing bowl. Stir in margarine and cocoa mixture. Blend well. Add vanilla, flour, nuts, if using, and salt. Pour into prepared pan and bake 30 to 40 minutes, or until a toothpick inserted in the center comes out clean.

For frosting, mix all ingredients together, spread over hot brownies, and serve.

Makes 20 servings.

Chicken Cordon Bleu Bites

Layered Green Salad

Boston Cream Poke Cake

Layered Green Salad

The flavors of this salad blend together perfectly! It's one of my family's favorites. —Kristen

1	head iceberg lettuce, chopped	4	tomatoes, chopped
2	cups baby spinach	1	bunch green onions, thinly sliced
	Salt and pepper, to taste	1	cup shredded cheddar cheese
10	hard-boiled eggs, chopped	1	(10-ounce) bag frozen peas, thawed
1	(12-ounce) package bacon, cooked and crumbled		

DRESSING

½	cup mayonnaise	2	tablespoons granulated sugar
½	cup sour cream		

In a large glass bowl, layer salad ingredients in order listed. Combine dressing ingredients in a separate bowl and whisk together until blended. Spread evenly over the peas. Cover and refrigerate up to 8 hours.

Makes 8 to 10 servings.

Chicken Cordon Bleu Bites

Our kids are huge chicken nugget fans, and my husband and I absolutely love chicken cordon bleu, so I thought it would be wonderful to combine our two favorites into one delicious bite of heavenly goodness. —Kristen

NUGGETS

5 boneless, skinless chicken breasts	½ cup all-purpose flour
8 ounces Swiss cheese, sliced	1 (6-ounce) box chicken stuffing mix, finely ground (or use Italian style bread crumbs)
7.5 ounces sliced ham	
3 eggs	1 recipe Honey Mustard Dipping Sauce
1 teaspoon water	

Preheat oven to 350 degrees F. Cut chicken breasts into thin, 1½-inch squares (if breasts are thick, slice them in half to thin them out). Cut cheese and ham slices into 1-inch squares. Sandwich cheese and ham between 2 slices of chicken. Poke a toothpick through the center of the stacked items. (The toothpick holds everything together when rolling the items in the flour, egg, and crumb mixtures.)

Beat eggs with 1 teaspoon water in a shallow bowl. Place flour in a separate shallow bowl, and bread crumbs in another bowl. Dip the cordon bleu bite in the flour mixture, then roll in the beaten egg mixture, and roll in the stuffing crumbs. Set on a greased cookie sheet. Slide the toothpick carefully out of the bite after placing it on the cookie sheet. After you have dipped all of the bites, spray them with butter-flavored cooking spray.

Bake, uncovered, 20 minutes. Serve with honey mustard dipping sauce.

Makes about 24 bites.

HONEY MUSTARD DIPPING SAUCE

1	tablespoon yellow mustard
1	tablespoon Dijon mustard
¼	cup honey
½	tablespoon lemon juice
⅛	teaspoon onion powder
⅓	cup mayonnaise

Combine all ingredients until well blended. Keep refrigerated until ready to serve.

Boston Cream Poke Cake

This is my favorite treat to take to a party. It tastes like you slaved all day making a delicious cake, when really it hardly takes any time at all! –Kristen

1 (18.25-ounce) box yellow cake mix and ingredients listed on box

2 (3.4-ounce) boxes instant vanilla or French vanilla pudding

4 cups milk

1 container chocolate frosting (or your favorite homemade chocolate frosting)

Make cake mix according to directions and bake in a well-greased 9x13-inch pan. Remove from oven.

While baked cake is still warm, poke holes all over the top, using a wooden spoon handle or other similarly sized object. You want the holes big enough that the pudding will seep in. In a medium bowl, add milk to pudding mixes and whisk until most of the lumps are removed. Pour pudding on top of warm cake, making sure to pour straight into the holes.

Spread remaining pudding evenly across the top of the cake, edge to edge. (Press down very gently to ensure that pudding goes into the holes.)

Put cake in fridge and allow to cool completely before frosting (about 2 hours).

Remove the lid and foil covering from the tub of frosting and microwave for 10 to 15 seconds. Stir frosting; it should still be thick, but pourable. Pour chocolate frosting on top of pudding.

Spread frosting evenly over cake. Start in the middle and gently spread to the sides. Allow to cool for a few minutes, then chill in the fridge until set.

Makes 16 servings.

THANKFUL
TABLECLOTH

Like most families, we like to enjoy a big Thanksgiving feast every year. We go around the table and share something we are thankful for. We loved hearing everyone's comments so much that we decided to create a fun tradition out of it. We bought a large white tablecloth and some permanent markers and a tradition was born!

Each year, every family member writes something they are thankful for on the tablecloth. The kids love to draw pictures or trace their hands so they can compare them the next year!

It's fun to look back and see what each person was thankful for in previous years and to remember all your blessings.

We spread the tablecloth over the table and reminisce as we enjoy our delicious meal! —Elyse

WHAT YOU'LL NEED

- **A large white tablecloth**
- **Several permanent markers of different colors**

Tomato Tortellini Soup

Cheddar Cheese Biscuits

Cherry Chocolate Nut Bars

Tomato Tortellini Soup

This recipe is perfect for a cold winter night. The best thing about it is that no one will ever know you used basic ingredients to make such a creamy and delectable soup! I often use fat-free half-and-half and skim milk, and the soup still tastes rich and creamy. —Stephanie

- 1 (9-ounce) package frozen or refrigerated cheese tortellini
- 2 (10.75-ounce) cans condensed tomato soup
- 2 cups chicken broth
- 2 cups milk
- 2 cups half-and-half
- ½ cup chopped oil-packed sun-dried tomatoes
- 1 teaspoon onion powder
- 1 teaspoon garlic powder
- 1 teaspoon dried basil
- ½ teaspoon salt
- ½ cup shredded Parmesan cheese

Cook tortellini according to package directions.

Meanwhile, in a large stockpot, combine soup, broth, milk, half-and-half, tomatoes, and seasonings. Heat through, stirring frequently. Drain tortellini and carefully add to soup. Stir in cheese. Sprinkle each serving with additional cheese if desired.

Makes about 8 servings.

Cheddar Cheese Biscuits

These cheddar-loaded biscuits take only minutes to put together but taste like you've spent hours on them. They are light, fluffy, and full of flavor!

2½ cups Bisquick baking mix

4 tablespoons cold butter

1 cup shredded cheddar cheese

¾ cup cold whole milk

¼ teaspoon garlic powder

TOPPING

2 tablespoons butter, melted

½ teaspoon garlic powder

¼ teaspoon dried parsley flakes

Pinch salt

Preheat oven to 400 degrees F. In a medium mixing bowl, combine Bisquick and cold butter using a fork or pastry cutter. Don't combine too thoroughly. There should be small chunks of butter in your mixture. Mix in cheese, milk, and garlic powder by hand, only until combined. Drop ¼-cup portions onto an ungreased baking sheet. Bake 15 to 17 minutes, or until golden brown.

In a small bowl, combine melted butter, garlic powder, parsley, and salt. Brush the garlic butter on top of the hot biscuits.

Makes 12 biscuits.

Cherry Chocolate Nut Bars

Our neighbor makes these bars every year for Christmas. If you are not home when they are delivered, you have to wait a whole year for another shot at these yummy bars! We finally got the recipe from her and are excited to share it here.

2 cups milk chocolate chips

¾ cup crunchy peanut butter

1½ cups salted peanuts, chopped

1 (10.5-ounce) package miniature marshmallows

1 (16-ounce) container cherry frosting

Melt chocolate chips and peanut butter on low power in the microwave. Stir well and add chopped peanuts. Spread half of the chocolate mixture in a 9x13-inch glass pan sprayed very lightly with cooking spray. Refrigerate 20 minutes.

Melt marshmallows in the microwave on low power, stirring every 20 seconds. When melted and smooth, stir in the frosting. Spread this mixture carefully on top of the chocolate layer. Let cool in the fridge for 30 minutes. Top with remaining chocolate. If chocolate has set up a little, microwave it for about 30 seconds on low power and stir well. Be sure to spread each layer to the edges of the pan.

Refrigerate until firm. Cut into pieces and store in refrigerator.

Makes about 48 pieces.

MENU 18

Personal Grilled-Chicken Alfredo Pizza

BLT Salad

No-Bake Peanut Butter Corn Flake Bars

BLT Salad

BLTs are the go-to sandwich around our house, and the salad version is just as delicious. —Kristen

6 strips bacon	½ cup mayonnaise
1 package premium romaine bagged salad	3 tablespoons granulated sugar
1 medium tomato, chopped	4 teaspoons apple cider vinegar
8 Monterey Jack cheese sticks, cut into cubes	1 teaspoon olive oil
	Salt and pepper, to taste
	1 cup croutons

Chop bacon into small pieces and cook in a large frying pan over medium heat, until crisp. Drain off fat and set bacon aside. In a large bowl, combine lettuce, tomato, and cheese. In a small mixing bowl, whisk together mayonnaise, sugar, vinegar, olive oil, and salt and pepper, to taste. Pour dressing over salad or serve on the side. Sprinkle with bacon and croutons.

Makes 4 to 6 servings.

Personal Grilled-Chicken Alfredo Pizza

We have pizza night every Friday at our house. My girls love the personal size and my husband loves the homemade sauce. You can't go wrong with these little pizzas! –Kristen

2 tablespoons unsalted butter

¼ teaspoon garlic powder

⅛ teaspoon onion powder

1 tablespoon all-purpose flour, plus more for dusting

½ cup plus 2 tablespoons heavy whipping cream or half-and-half

½ cup plus 2 tablespoons milk

½ cup shredded Parmesan cheese

Salt and pepper, to taste

1 (16-ounce) tube refrigerated pizza dough

1 cup shredded mozzarella cheese

1½ cups cubed cooked chicken

8 slices bacon, cooked and chopped

2 tablespoons chopped green onions

Preheat oven to 425 degrees F. To make alfredo, melt butter in a medium saucepan over medium heat. Whisk in garlic powder, onion powder, and flour and stir constantly for 1 minute. Slowly whisk in cream and milk. Bring mixture to a gentle bubble and allow to gently boil 20 seconds, stirring constantly. Remove from heat; add Parmesan, season with salt and pepper, to taste, and then return to warm heat, stirring occasionally until ready to use.

On a lightly floured surface, roll out pizza dough into three 5-inch round crusts. Place dough on a greased pizza pan or baking dish. Spread alfredo sauce over the dough, coming within about 1 inch of the edge. Sprinkle on the mozzarella and top with chicken, bacon, and green onion. Bake 14 to 16 minutes, or until crust is golden brown. Cut into slices and serve.

Makes three 5-inch pizzas.

No-Bake Peanut Butter Corn Flake Bars

I love no-bake recipes, especially when the weather starts warming up. The last thing I want to do on a nice day is spend all day in the kitchen. These bars take only a few minutes to make and are a delicious treat. —Lauren

1 **cup crunchy peanut butter**	3 **cups crushed corn flakes**
½ **cup granulated sugar**	2 **cups milk chocolate chips**
½ **cup light corn syrup**	

Heat peanut butter, sugar, and corn syrup in a large saucepan over medium heat until melted. Remove pan from heat and stir in crushed corn flakes. Press mixture into a greased 8x11-inch pan. Melt chocolate chips in a microwave-safe bowl in 30-second increments until melted. Stir chocolate until smooth and spread on top of peanut butter mixture. Let cool until firm.

Makes 15 bars.

MENU 19

Crunchy Black Bean Tacos

Creamed Corn

Gooey Lemon Bars

Creamed Corn

We never had creamed corn growing up, so I always assumed it didn't taste good. After I got married, my husband introduced me to creamed corn, and I have never turned back! Forget the canned version—this recipe tastes a million times better. —Elyse

◇◇

2   (20-ounce) packages frozen corn kernels

1   cup heavy whipping cream

1   cup milk

1   teaspoon salt

2   teaspoons granulated sugar

⅛   teaspoon white pepper

2   tablespoons butter, melted

2   tablespoons all-purpose flour

Combine frozen corn kernels, cream, milk, salt, sugar, and white pepper in a large pot and bring to a boil. Meanwhile, whisk together melted butter and flour until combined and add to the corn mixture. Mix well and remove from heat.

Makes 6 to 8 servings.

Crunchy Black Bean Tacos

These tacos taste just like they came from a restaurant and are so easy to make!

1 (15-ounce) can black beans, drained and rinsed

½ cup minced red onion

1 teaspoon cumin

1 teaspoon paprika

2 tablespoons chopped cilantro

1 teaspoon oil

8 corn tortillas

1 cup shredded pepper Jack cheese

1 avocado, sliced

Salsa, for garnishing

Sour cream, for garnishing

In a medium bowl, combine beans, red onion, cumin, paprika, and cilantro. Heat a large, nonstick skillet over medium-high heat and coat with oil. Place one tortilla at a time on the hot skillet and add about ¼ cup of bean filling to one half of the tortilla. Top with a sprinkle of grated cheese. Use a spatula to carefully fold the tortilla over so it forms a shell. Press down lightly on the tortilla with the spatula so it holds its shape.

Cook each taco about 3 minutes per side, or until golden brown and crispy. Serve with avocado, salsa, sour cream, or any toppings you prefer.

Makes 8 tacos.

Gooey Lemon Bars

These are by far my favorite family recipe. Our mom has been making them for years. If you are a lemon lover like me, you have to give these a try. —Lauren

CRUST

1   (18.25-ounce) box lemon cake mix

½   cup butter

1   egg, slightly beaten

FILLING/FROSTING

2 to 3   cups powdered sugar

3 to 4   tablespoons butter, softened

1½   tablespoons lemon juice

3 to 5   drops yellow food coloring

1   (8-ounce) package cream cheese, room temperature

2   eggs

Preheat oven to 350 degrees F. Combine crust ingredients and mix with fork. Press down in a 9x13-inch pan with greased bottom. Set aside.

For filling, mix powdered sugar and butter with a hand mixer. Add enough lemon juice to form the consistency of thick frosting. Fold in cream cheese and yellow food coloring. Set aside 1 cup to spread on top after baking. Be sure to not skip this step! Add eggs to remaining frosting mixture and beat until fluffy. Spread on top of cake mix in the pan and bake 25 to 30 minutes. Watch carefully so it doesn't over-bake. Let cool completely and then spread reserved frosting mixture on top.

Makes 20 bars.

Slow Cooker Chicken Noodle Soup

No-Knead Homemade Wheat Rolls

Gooey Almond and Coconut
Chex Mix

No-Knead Homemade Wheat Rolls

My family loves homemade rolls, but I am always intimidated when I read recipes with a long of list of directions. These rolls are foolproof, and you don't even have to knead them! —Camille

1 (.25-ounce) package active dry yeast, or 2¼ teaspoons yeast	1 cup whole wheat flour
1¼ cups warm water	2 tablespoons butter, softened
2 cups all-purpose flour	2 tablespoons honey
	1 teaspoon salt

In a large bowl, dissolve yeast in warm water. Add remaining ingredients. Beat on medium speed 3 minutes (dough will be sticky). Do not knead. Cover and let rise in a warm place until doubled, about 30 minutes.

Preheat oven to 375 degrees F. Stir dough down. Spray a muffin tin with nonstick cooking spray and fill each muffin cup half full with dough. Cover and let rise until doubled, about 15 minutes.

Bake 10 to 15 minutes, or until golden brown. Cool 1 minute before removing from pan to a wire rack.

Makes 12 rolls.

Slow Cooker Chicken Noodle Soup

This soup is so simple to make and tastes amazing. Prep it in the morning, and you can smell it simmering all day long. This is definitely one of my favorite soup recipes of all time. —Camille

5 cups chicken broth

1 (10.75-ounce) can 98 percent fat-free cream of chicken soup

½ onion, finely chopped

2 to 3 ribs celery, finely chopped

4 large carrots, finely chopped

½ cup sliced green onions

1 (15-ounce) can corn, drained

½ teaspoon garlic powder

Salt and pepper, to taste

1½ cups egg noodles, uncooked

2 cups chopped or shredded cooked chicken (or 2 cans canned cooked chicken)

Add everything but the noodles and cooked chicken to the slow cooker. Cook on low heat 6 hours. Add the uncooked noodles and cooked chicken, turn heat to high, and cook 1 more hour. Serve and enjoy!

Makes 4 servings.

Gooey Almond and Coconut Chex Mix

This recipe was a staple in our house every holiday season while we were growing up. It's easy to throw together, the kids can help make it, and it's ready to eat in less than 15 minutes. —Camille

1   (14- to 17-ounce) box Rice or Corn Chex cereal

1   (7-ounce) bag sweetened, shredded coconut

1   (5-ounce) bag almonds (about 1⅓ cup)

1½   cups granulated sugar

¾   cup margarine or butter

1¼   cups light corn syrup

Pinch salt

Spray a very large bowl with nonstick cooking spray. Pour in the entire box of Chex cereal, coconut, and almonds. Gently mix together. (This is the perfect job for your kids to do.)

Mix together sugar, butter, light corn syrup, and pinch of salt in a medium saucepan over high heat. Bring to a full boil, turn heat down to medium, and cook three minutes, stirring constantly. Pour over cereal mixture in the big bowl and stir evenly.

Spread cereal evenly on waxed paper and let cool (though it's delicious to eat while warm, too!). Once it cools, bag it up in little cellophane bags and share with neighbors and friends. You can also store it in an airtight container or resealable bag and it lasts for a couple of days.

Makes 8 servings.

Honey BBQ Meatloaf

Creamy Slow Cooker Mashed Potatoes

Butterfinger Blondies

Creamy Slow Cooker Mashed Potatoes

These mashed potatoes are some of the creamiest and most flavorful I have ever had. I think letting them slow cook for a couple of hours makes the flavors really soak in. My family raves about them. —Camille

5 pounds red potatoes, scrubbed, peeled, and cut into chunks	1 (8-ounce) package cream cheese, softened
1 tablespoon minced garlic, or to taste	¼ cup butter
3 cubes chicken bouillon	Salt and pepper, to taste
1 (8-ounce) container sour cream	

In a large pot of lightly salted boiling water, cook potatoes, garlic, and bouillon until potatoes are tender but still firm, about 15 minutes. Drain, reserving water. In a bowl, mash potatoes with sour cream and cream cheese, adding reserved water as needed to attain desired consistency.

Transfer potato mixture to a slow cooker, cover, and cook on low heat 2 to 3 hours. Just before serving, stir in butter and season with salt and pepper, to taste.

Makes 4 to 6 servings.

Honey BBQ Meatloaf

The combination of honey and barbecue is definitely comfort food at its finest. This is one meatloaf recipe that will please even your pickiest eaters!

1½ to 2 pounds ground beef

1 cup quick-cooking oats

2 eggs

2 tablespoons Worcestershire sauce

1 tablespoon spicy brown mustard

½ cup barbecue sauce

1 tablespoon honey

Salt and pepper, to taste

TOPPING

¼ cup barbecue sauce

1 tablespoon honey

2 teaspoons Worcestershire sauce

Preheat oven to 350 degrees F. In a large bowl, mix together ground beef, oats, eggs, Worcestershire sauce, mustard, barbecue sauce, honey, salt, and pepper. (I've found that it's easiest to use my hands to mix it all together.) When completely combined, mold meat into a large mound and place in a loaf pan sprayed with nonstick cooking spray.

In a small bowl, whisk together topping ingredients and spread half on top of the meatloaf. Reserve the other half for serving. Bake 50 to 60 minutes, until internal temperature registers 160 degrees F on a meat thermometer. Remove from oven and let cool 5 to 10 minutes. Slice and drizzle remaining sauce on top.

Makes 6 servings.

Butterfinger Blondies

Since this makes so many blondies, many of our neighbors have had the chance to try these and even months later, they are still raving about them! These are as amazing as they sound.

1 cup unsalted butter, softened	2½ cups all-purpose flour
1 cup light brown sugar	1 teaspoon baking soda
½ cup granulated sugar	1 teaspoon coarse sea salt
2 teaspoons vanilla extract	2 cups coarsely chopped Butterfinger Bars (about 16 Fun Size bars)
2 eggs	1 recipe Butterfinger Buttercream

Preheat oven to 350 degrees F. Cream butter and sugars in mixing bowl. Add vanilla and eggs, and mix until incorporated.

With mixer on low speed, add flour, baking soda, and salt until just combined. Stir in chopped Butterfingers. Spread batter in a 9×13-inch baking dish and bake 25 minutes until center is just set. Remove from oven and cool completely. Prepare Butterfinger Buttercream and spread on cooled bars.

Makes 15 servings.

BUTTERFINGER BUTTERCREAM

½ cup butter, room temperature

½ cup vegetable shortening

2½ to 3 cups powdered sugar

½ cup chopped Butterfinger Bars (about 4 Fun Size bars)

Cream butter and shortening together until smooth. On low speed, mix in powdered sugar; increase mixer speed to medium and mix until smooth. Stir in chopped Butterfingers.

Monterey Chicken

Honey-Lime Fruit Salad

Graham Cracker Monster Cookies

Honey-Lime Fruit Salad

This salad is easy to throw together, and it tastes amazing. It is really the perfect side dish to any summer meal! —Stephanie

1	(20-ounce) can pineapple chunks, drained well	1	cup halved grapes
1	(4-ounce) can mandarin oranges, drained well	1	cup quartered strawberries
			Zest from one lime, about 1 tablespoon
2 to 3	ripe kiwis, peeled and sliced	1	teaspoon poppy seeds (optional)
		2	tablespoons honey

Combine fruit in a medium-large serving bowl. Add lime zest and poppy seeds, toss gently. Drizzle honey over fruit and gently mix, until fruit is evenly coated with honey. Serve.

Note: This fruit salad is best served right away (or at least within an hour of making) because the strawberries tend to stain the pale-colored fruit. It doesn't affect the taste at all, but it can affect the presentation.

Makes 6 servings.

Monterey Chicken

This dish can be made in under 30 minutes and tastes incredible.

4 to 6 boneless, skinless chicken breasts, thawed	**1½** cups shredded Monterey Jack and cheddar cheese mix
Salt and pepper, to taste	Fresh diced tomatoes, for garnishing
1 cup barbecue sauce	Diced green onions, for garnishing
10 strips bacon, cooked	

Place chicken breasts between plastic wrap and pound with a meat mallet or rolling pin until they are flat. Season with salt and pepper.

Cook the chicken on an outdoor grill over medium-high heat, 4 to 5 minutes per side, or until fully cooked. Internal temperature should reach 165 degrees F.

After chicken is finished cooking, transfer to a large baking sheet covered in aluminum foil. Spread 2 to 3 tablespoons barbecue sauce over each chicken breast. Top each chicken breast with 2 slices cooked bacon and a handful of the shredded cheese mix. Place the baking sheet under oven's broiler long enough to melt the cheese. Top with diced tomatoes and green onions. Serve immediately.

Makes 4 to 6 servings.

Graham Cracker Monster Cookies

Without needing eggs, this recipe combines graham crackers, sweetened condensed milk, and chocolate chips to make an amazingly moist and delicious treat!

1½ cups graham crackers, finely crushed

¾ cup all-purpose flour

2 teaspoons baking powder

1 (14–ounce) can sweetened condensed milk

½ cup butter or margarine, softened

2 cups milk chocolate chips

1 cup chopped walnuts

1 cup flaked coconut (optional)

1 teaspoon vanilla extract

Preheat oven to 350 degrees F.

In a medium bowl, mix together graham cracker crumbs, flour, and baking powder. In another mixing bowl, beat sweetened condensed milk and softened butter until smooth. Then add in vanilla extract.

Add crumb mixture and stir until smooth. Add chocolate chips and coconut.

Roll into 1½-inch balls or drop spoonfuls onto a lightly greased cookie sheet.

Bake 12 minutes or until lightly browned. Let cool 5 minutes on cookie sheet then remove to finish cooling on wire rack.

Makes 36 cookies.

52 WEEKS OF FOOD STORAGE

This list is meant to be a guideline to help you begin building your food storage. Be sure to buy food that your family will eat, taking into account any special diet or allergy needs. For more information on expanding your food storage, see the following websites:

- www.ready.gov/food
- http://www.bt.cdc.gov/preparedness/kit/food/
- www.foodinsurance.com

It never hurts to be prepared, and a small supply is better than no supply at all!

I remember how every year we would go with our dad to the grocery store's huge case-lot sale. We would stock up on all of our food storage items for an entire year. My dad created a big, rolling shelf system in one of our basement storage rooms, and we would rotate through all of the food during the course of the year. It was a lot of work, and a big expense to buy everything all at once. Now, as we have tried to establish food storage in our own homes, we realize how hard it is to shop for what we need all at once.

We created this list of food storage staples that you can collect for 52 weeks. We recommend adding items slowly to your shopping list each week, buying one or two items. Start small, and before you know it, you will be well on your way to a solid supply of food. –Stephanie

WHAT YOU'LL NEED

Week 1: Water—two gallons per person. You can fill up your own sanitized containers, or buy them.

Week 2: One case of canned tomato soup.

Week 3: Plastic plates, bowls, and utensils.

Week 4: Salt—one pound per person.

Week 5: Oats—two pounds per person. Store two more gallons of water per person.

Week 6: Peanut butter—one pound per person.

Week 7: Sugar—two pounds per person.

Week 8: Two cases of canned evaporated milk.

Week 9: Three pounds of pasta.

Week 10: Four jars of jam or jelly. Store two more gallons of water per person.

Week 11: Flour—five pounds per person.

Week 12: Two large bottles of vinegar.

Week 13: Two large bottles of vegetable oil.

Week 14: One case of canned applesauce.

Week 15: Three pounds of pasta. Store two more gallons of water per person.

Week 16: Honey—one and a half pounds per person. Store two or more gallons of water per person.

Week 17: One case of canned olives.

Week 18: One case of canned chicken noodle soup. Store two or more gallons of water per person.

Week 19: Four jars of mayonnaise and one box of protein bars.

Week 20: Five pounds of rice. Store two more gallons of water per person.

Week 21: Sugar—two pounds per person.

Week 22: Four boxes of baking soda, and eight cans of tuna.

Week 23: Peanut butter—one pound per person.

Week 24: Oats—three pounds per person.

Week 25: One case of canned tomatoes. Store two more gallons of water per person.

Week 26: Salt—one pound per person.

Week 27: Two loaves of bread (to store in your freezer).

Week 28: Four cans of baking powder.

Week 29: One large package (or can) of dried fruit.

Week 30: Three pounds of dried beans. Store two more gallons of water per person.

Week 31: Two bottles of ketchup and two bottles of mustard.

Week 32: Four pounds of powdered sugar.

Week 33: Oats—three pounds per person.

Week 34: One case of canned pineapple.

Week 35: One case of canned corn. Store two more gallons of water per person.

Week 36: Sugar—two pounds per person.

Week 37: Three pounds of brown sugar.

Week 38: One case of canned cream of chicken soup.

Week 39: Six boxes of macaroni and cheese.

Week 40: One case of canned mandarin oranges.

Week 41: Honey—one and a half pounds per person. Store two more gallons of water per person.

Week 42: Five pounds of rice.

Week 43: Three pounds of pasta.

Week 44: Salt—one pound per person.

Week 45: One case of canned black beans

Week 46: One case of canned cream of mushroom soup. Store two more gallons of water per person.

Week 47: Flour—five pounds per person.

Week 48: Five cans of pasta sauce.

Week 49: One gallon of bleach and one manual can opener.

Week 50: Two pounds of your favorite powdered drink mix.

Week 51: One case of canned green beans. Store two more gallons of water per person.

Week 52: One case of canned chili.

Three-Cheese Mushroom and Spinach Calzones

Oven-Roasted Parmesan Broccoli

Berry Cheesecake Pudding

Berry Cheesecake Pudding

Some of you will say this is really a dessert; but if you have a crazy sweet tooth like mine, you can call it an amazing salad. This dish is a huge hit at any potluck and makes a lot if you need to feed a crowd. I promise you won't have any leftovers! —Kristen

1   (32-ounce) container low-fat strawberry yogurt

2   (3-ounce) boxes instant cheesecake pudding

1   (16-ounce) container light nondairy whipped topping, thawed

1   (16-ounce) bag frozen mixed berries, partially thawed

3   large bananas, sliced

1   pound fresh strawberries, sliced

Pour yogurt into a large bowl and mix in pudding (it will be kind of lumpy). Fold in whipped topping and stir until all lumps are gone. Add all of the fruit and stir to combine. Keep refrigerated.

Makes 6 to 8 servings.

Three-Cheese Mushroom and Spinach Calzones

I'm usually the only person in our family who eats mushrooms and spinach, but this recipe changed all that!
—Kristen

1 tablespoon olive oil, plus more for brushing

1 (8-ounce) package sliced mushrooms

2 cloves garlic, minced

½ teaspoon dried oregano

4 cups (packed) fresh baby spinach

   Salt and pepper, to taste

1 (13.8-ounce) tube refrigerated pizza dough

5 tablespoons grated Parmesan cheese, divided

1½ cups grated Fontina cheese, divided

¼ cup ricotta cheese

¼ teaspoon crushed red pepper

   Nonstick cooking spray

Preheat oven to 425 degrees F. Heat 1 tablespoon oil in a large skillet over medium-high heat. Add mushrooms and sauté until browned, about 5 minutes. Add garlic and oregano and stir 1 minute. Add spinach and stir, until just wilted, about 1 minute. Transfer ingredients from the skillet to a medium bowl. Season with salt and pepper.

Spray a baking sheet with nonstick cooking spray. Roll out dough on baking sheet to a 15x10-inch rectangle. Sprinkle 3 tablespoons Parmesan cheese onto one half of the crust, leaving a 1-inch border around the edge. (It is easier to seal if nothing is close to the edge.) Sprinkle on ¾ cup Fontina cheese, and the mushroom mixture over that. Sprinkle 2 tablespoons Parmesan and ¾ cup Fontina over the mushrooms. Spoon dollops of ricotta cheese on top and sprinkle with crushed red pepper. Fold the empty half of dough over the filled side. Crimp the edges with a fork to seal. Brush the top of the calzone with olive oil.

Bake until brown, about 18 minutes.

Makes 5 servings.

Oven-Roasted Parmesan Broccoli

There is something about cooked broccoli and cheese that makes my mouth water. This is such a quick and easy side dish to prepare. The best part is that my kids will eat it! —Kristen

2 **cups chopped broccoli florets**	½ **teaspoon garlic salt**
¼ **cup olive oil**	⅓ **cup shredded fresh Parmesan cheese**

Preheat oven to 400 degrees F. Place broccoli in a large bowl and drizzle oil on top. Toss to coat. Sprinkle garlic salt on top and mix to incorporate.

Spread broccoli on a large baking sheet covered with aluminum foil and bake about 15 minutes, until it starts to turn golden brown (you want it to toast, but not burn).

Pour broccoli back into a bowl as soon as you pull it out of the oven and mix with cheese. Serve immediately.

Makes 2 to 4 servings.

Homemade Turkey Meatball Subs

Baked Zucchini Fries

M&M's Cookie Pie

M&M's Cookie Pie

If you are looking for a tasty snack to curb your sweet tooth cravings, this M&M's cookie pie is the perfect fix! This sweet treat is even better when topped with ice cream and chocolate syrup.

¾ cup butter, room temperature

½ cup light brown sugar

1 egg

1 teaspoon vanilla extract

1 cup plus 1 tablespoon all-purpose flour

¼ teaspoon baking soda

1½ cups mini M&M's

Preheat oven to 325 degrees F. Grease a 9½-inch pie plate; set aside. In a large mixing bowl, cream together butter and brown sugar. Add in egg and vanilla and mix well. In a separate bowl, combine flour and baking soda. Add flour mixture to batter and mix until completely incorporated. Fold in M&M's. Pour and spread batter into prepared pie pan and bake 25 to 30 minutes, or until a toothpick comes out clean. Let cool and cut into slices.

Makes 8 servings.

Homemade Turkey Meatball Subs

My family loves meatballs. I used to go the easy route and use frozen ones . . . until I found these! It is worth every bit of extra time to make them. —Elyse

1 pound ground turkey

½ cup dried bread crumbs

1 teaspoon dried basil

1 teaspoon dried oregano

1 teaspoon dried parsley

½ teaspoon garlic salt

½ cup grated Parmesan cheese

1 egg

2 tablespoons olive oil

1 tablespoon Montreal steak seasoning

1 (24-ounce) jar marinara sauce

16 slices provolone cheese

8 buns or sandwich rolls, split

Preheat oven to 425 degrees F. In a large bowl, mix together turkey, bread crumbs, basil, oregano, parsley, garlic salt, Parmesan cheese, egg, olive oil, and steak seasoning. Form meat mixture into 1½-inch meatballs and place on a greased cookie sheet. Bake 15 minutes, or until cooked through. (Internal temperature should reach 160 degrees F.)

Place split buns on a baking tray and top each half with 2 slices provolone cheese. Preheat oven to broil and lightly toast buns until golden brown and cheese has melted.

Warm marinara sauce in a large saucepan over low-medium heat or in the microwave, until heated through.

Top the bottom half of each toasted bun with 3 to 4 meatballs, cover in marinara sauce and replace the top half of each bun.

Makes 8 sandwiches.

Baked Zucchini Fries

It seems like the older my little boy gets, the pickier he becomes! He used to eat any fruit or vegetable, but now I have to beg him to eat just a bite or two. Except when I serve these wonderful, dip-able fries. —Elyse

½ **cup panko bread crumbs**

¼ **cup grated Parmesan cheese**

2 **eggs**

3 **medium zucchini (about 1 pound)**

Preheat oven to 425 degrees F. Line a baking sheet with aluminum foil and spray with nonstick cooking spray. Set aside. Combine bread crumbs and Parmesan cheese. Set aside. Whisk eggs together in a shallow pie plate and set aside.

Cut off the ends of the zucchini and then cut the zucchini in half so you have two stubby pieces. Set one piece on its end and cut it in half lengthwise. Cut that half in half, making 2 planks. Repeat with the remaining halves. (You'll get 16 planks per zucchini.)

Stack 2 planks on top of each other and cut into strips. Thicker strips will yield bigger fries with more zucchini flavor while thin strips will be crispy and taste virtually nothing like zucchini. When all the fries are cut, blot the pieces with a paper towel.

With a small handful at a time, dip zucchini sticks in the egg, shake them to remove any excess, and then roll each one in about 2 to 3 tablespoons of bread crumbs at a time, adding crumbs as needed. You don't want to work with all the bread crumbs at once or they soak up moisture from the egg and won't stick to the zucchini. Place coated strips on the prepared baking sheet and repeat for all zucchini strips.

Bake 10 to 12 minutes, remove from oven, flip the fries, and bake another 10 to 12 minutes, or until zucchini coating is crisp and golden brown. Serve immediately with marinara sauce or ranch dressing.

Makes 8 servings.

DIY MENU BOARD

What's for dinner?" is a common question at my house. So I decided to make a cute menu board to decorate my home and answer everyone's favorite question at the same time!

I love being able to plan ahead and know what we are having for dinner, and this menu board does the trick! —Elyse

WHAT YOU'LL NEED

- **Any size picture frame**
- **Krylon Spray Paint (any color)**
- **Rust-Oleum Chalkboard Spray Paint**
- **Adhesive or vinyl letters for each day of the week**

INSTRUCTIONS

1. Buy a rectangular frame. I found one on clearance that was perfect for this project, but you can use any size frame you want.

2. Take the frame apart and paint it with Krylon Spray Paint. (I liked the jade color, but you can pick your favorite color.) If you already like the original frame, you don't need to worry about painting it.

3. Remove the cardboard backing and glass from the frame. Cut a piece of wood the same size as the glass and spray paint it with Rust-Oleum Chalkboard Spray Paint. Spray on at least three coats of paint, letting each coat dry completely before applying the next one.

4. After the chalkboard is completely dry, replace the wood board and cardboard backing into the frame.

5. Turn the frame over and attach either adhesive or vinyl letter stickers for each day of the week to the front of your board. You can also write the letters on with chalk, if you prefer.

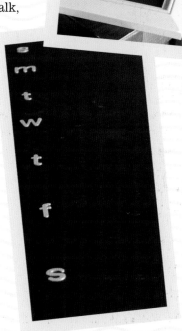

Baked Coconut Shrimp

Mom's Broccoli Salad

Garlic Roasted Potatoes

Baked Coconut Shrimp

I am a huge fan of shrimp, and I love battered coconut shrimp. This baked version tastes just as good as (if not better than!) fried shrimp—with fewer calories! —Stephanie

1 pound peeled, deveined large shrimp	¾ teaspoon cayenne pepper
⅓ cup cornstarch	2 cups sweetened, flaked coconut
1 teaspoon salt	3 egg whites

Preheat oven to 400 degrees F. Lightly coat a baking sheet with cooking spray. Rinse and pat dry the peeled and deveined shrimp. In one bowl, mix cornstarch, salt, and cayenne pepper. In another bowl, beat egg whites until foamy. Pour coconut in a third bowl. Holding one shrimp by the tail, coat it in the cornstarch mixture (covering it completely), then dip it in the egg mixture, and then roll it in the coconut. Place it on the baking sheet and repeat until you run out of mixture. (I completely coat about 30 shrimp.)

Bake 15 to 20 minutes, flipping halfway through, until shrimp is pink on the outside and coconut is lightly browned.

Serve with your favorite cocktail sauce.

Makes 6 servings.

Mom's Broccoli Salad

This broccoli salad recipe is our absolute favorite! We have tweaked it a few times to get it just right. It's so easy to make and a great salad to serve year-round. It shows up at summer barbecues as well as our Christmas parties!

1   cup light mayonnaise

2   tablespoons red wine vinegar

½   cup granulated sugar

½   teaspoon salt

1   pound fresh broccoli (about 2 bunches), cut into small florets

1   medium red onion

1   cup grated cheddar cheese

8   strips bacon, cooked crisp and crumbled

½   cup sunflower seeds

¾   cup Craisins

Prepare dressing in advance to let flavors meld while chilling in the refrigerator. To make dressing, whisk together mayonnaise, vinegar, sugar, and salt, until sugar is dissolved. Cover and chill at least 1 hour.

In a large bowl combine broccoli, onion, and grated cheese. Toss with bacon pieces, sunflower seeds, and Craisins. Toss with dressing to coat before serving.

Makes 6 servings.

Garlic Roasted Potatoes

This is the perfect side dish to almost any meal. It is simple to make and is absolutely delicious!

3 pounds small red potatoes, washed but not peeled

¼ cup olive oil

1½ teaspoons salt

1 teaspoon black pepper

2 tablespoons minced garlic (about 6 cloves)

2 tablespoons minced fresh parsley

Preheat oven to 400 degrees F. Cut potatoes into 1-inch cubes and place in a bowl with olive oil, salt, pepper, and garlic. Toss until potatoes are well coated. Spread potatoes on a baking sheet and roast 45 minutes, or until browned and crisp. Flip twice with a spatula during cooking so they will brown on all sides.

After removing potatoes from oven, toss with parsley, season to taste, and serve hot.

Makes 6 servings.

MENU 26

Overnight Caramel French Toast

Egg Soufflé

Strawberry Sunrise Drink

Strawberry Sunrise Drink

Sometimes plain orange juice just doesn't cut it. We decided to add some of our favorite fruits to give this orange juice a little something extra. This is perfect for breakfast, or to go along with any meal.

½ pound strawberries, washed and hulled

½ pound pineapple, peeled and chopped

½ banana

2 cups orange juice

6 large ice cubes

Cut up fruit and place in the blender. Add orange juice and ice cubes. Blend about 30 seconds, or until all of the fruit and ice is blended and mixed with the juice.

Makes 4 servings.

Overnight Caramel French Toast

We love that we can prepare this the night before and have it ready in 20 minutes the next morning.

TOPPING

1 cup packed light brown sugar

6 tablespoons butter or margarine

⅓ cup heavy whipping cream

1 tablespoon light corn syrup

1 cup chopped pecans (optional)

FRENCH TOAST

3 eggs

½ cup milk

1 teaspoon vanilla extract

¼ teaspoon salt

8 (¾-inch-thick) diagonal-cut slices French bread

Whipped topping (optional)

Spray 9x13-inch glass baking dish with cooking spray and set aside. In a 2-quart saucepan, mix topping ingredients. Cook over medium heat, stirring constantly, until smooth. Do not boil. Spread in baking dish.

In a shallow bowl, beat eggs with fork. Beat in milk, vanilla, and salt. Dip bread slices into egg mixture, making sure all egg mixture is absorbed; arrange over topping in dish. Cover and refrigerate at least 8 hours or overnight.

When ready to bake, heat oven to 400 degrees F. Uncover baking dish and bake 20 to 25 minutes, or until bubbly and toast is golden brown. Remove from oven and let stand 3 minutes.

Place large, heatproof serving platter upside down over baking dish and invert platter and baking dish. Remove baking dish, scraping any extra caramel topping onto toast. Serve immediately, with whipped topping if desired.

Makes 6 servings.

Egg Soufflé

Our mom made this delicious soufflé for us growing up, and it is still a favorite today. This fluffy egg soufflé is filled with fresh veggies for the perfect breakfast dish.

2 tablespoons butter or margarine	⅛ cup chopped onion
6 eggs	⅛ cup chopped green bell pepper
⅓ cup sour cream	⅛ cup chopped red bell pepper
⅓ cup milk	½ cup sliced fresh mushrooms, sautéed (or canned)
½ teaspoon salt	¾ cup shredded Colby Jack cheese

Preheat oven to 325 degrees F. Melt butter in a 6x6-inch baking dish. In a medium bowl, beat together eggs, sour cream, milk, and salt. Stir in onion, green pepper, red pepper, mushrooms, and cheese. Pour into buttered baking dish and bake, uncovered, 35 to 45 minutes, until soufflé is golden brown and the middle is firm.

This recipe can easily be doubled or tripled. Just use a larger baking dish.

Makes 6 servings.

MENU 27

Homemade Chicken Nuggets

Slow Cooker Macaroni and Cheese

Applesauce Oatmeal Cookies

Slow Cooker Macaroni and Cheese

Macaroni and cheese is one of my favorite foods of all time. I love both the homemade versions and the easy versions that can be made in your microwave in 3½ minutes and only require you to add water. This recipe is a little of both: homemade, but easy, and incredibly delicious. —Camille

2 cups uncooked elbow macaroni	½ teaspoon salt
4 tablespoons butter	1 cup milk
2½ cups grated sharp cheddar cheese	½ teaspoon dry mustard
½ cup sour cream	½ teaspoon black pepper
1 (10.75-ounce) can condensed cheddar cheese soup	

Boil the macaroni 6 minutes and drain. In a medium saucepan over medium-high heat, melt butter and cheese until the cheese melts, stirring constantly. Spray slow cooker with nonstick cooking spray. Combine cheese mixture, sour cream, soup, salt, milk, mustard and pepper in slow cooker. Add the drained macaroni and stir again. Cook on low 2 to 2½ hours, stirring occasionally.

Makes 6 servings.

Homemade Chicken Nuggets

Frozen chicken nuggets were a staple in my life growing up. This homemade version is always a hit with my kids—and my husband. It comes together quite quickly, and I feel great serving something homemade. It also doubles well. —Camille

1	pound boneless, skinless chicken breasts	¼	teaspoon onion powder
3	cups corn flakes	¼	teaspoon garlic powder
⅓	cup grated Parmesan cheese		Pinch black pepper
½	teaspoon salt	2	eggs, beaten
		¼	cup all-purpose flour

Cut chicken breasts into nugget-size pieces. Set aside. Preheat oven to 425 degrees F. Grease cookie sheet.

Put cereal in large resealable plastic bag and crush to a fine texture. Pour flakes into medium bowl and stir in Parmesan cheese, salt, onion powder, garlic powder, and pepper.

Place eggs in separate small bowl.

Place flour in separate small bowl.

To bread chicken, coat chicken piece in flour, shaking off excess. Dip in the egg, and then coat in corn flake mixture.

Arrange chicken on prepared baking sheet and bake until golden brown, 12 to 15 minutes.

Makes 4 servings.

Applesauce Oatmeal Cookies

If you are looking for a way to spend more time with your kids, baking together in the kitchen is a good place to start. And you can never go wrong with applesauce cookies. —Camille

- 1 cup unsweetened applesauce
- 1 cup light brown sugar
- ½ cup butter, softened
- 1 egg
- 2 cups all-purpose flour
- 1 cup quick-cooking oats

- ½ teaspoon salt
- 1 teaspoon baking soda
- 1 teaspoon ground cinnamon
- ½ teaspoon ground nutmeg
- ½ teaspoon ground cloves
- 1 cup semi-sweet chocolate chips (optional)

Preheat oven to 375 degrees. Mix together applesauce, brown sugar, butter, and egg. Add remaining ingredients (except chocolate chips) and stir until combined. Dough should be firm (add more flour if it isn't). Fold in chocolate chips and scoop heaping tablespoonfuls onto a greased cookie sheet. Bake 13 to 15 minutes, until golden brown on top.

Makes about 3 dozen cookies.

MENU 28

Slow Cooker Glazed Pork Loin

Homemade Applesauce

German Chocolate Cake Cookies

Homemade Applesauce

This applesauce makes a great side dish or after-school snack.

◇◇

4 apples, peeled, cored, and chopped	¼ cup granulated sugar
¾ cup water	½ teaspoon ground cinnamon

In a medium saucepan, combine apples, water, sugar, and cinnamon. Cover and cook over medium heat 30 to 40 minutes, or until apples are soft. Allow to cool, then mash with a fork or potato masher. Refrigerate until ready to serve.

Makes 2 to 4 servings.

Slow Cooker Glazed Pork Loin

With the great combination of balsamic vinegar and brown sugar, this roast is so moist and flavorful.

1 teaspoon ground sage	1 clove garlic, crushed
½ teaspoon salt	1 (2-pound) boneless pork loin
¼ teaspoon black pepper	½ cup water

GLAZE

½ cup light brown sugar	½ cup water
1 tablespoon cornstarch	2 tablespoons soy sauce
¼ cup balsamic vinegar	

Combine sage, salt, pepper, and garlic. Rub over roast. Place in slow cooker with ½ cup water. Cook on low 6 to 8 hours. About 1 hour before roast is done, combine ingredients for glaze in small saucepan. Heat and stir until mixture thickens, about 10 to 15 minutes. Brush roast with glaze 2 or 3 times during the last hour of cooking. Serve with remaining glaze on the side.

Makes 4 to 6 servings.

German Chocolate Cake Cookies

These are some of Mom's best cookies! The cookie is moist and chewy, and we top it off with heavenly German Chocolate Frosting. This frosting is a no-fail recipe. We're lucky if the frosting makes it to the cookies.

1   (18.25-ounce) box German chocolate cake mix

⅔   cup butter flavor shortening

2   eggs

1   teaspoon water

1   recipe German Chocolate Frosting

Preheat oven to 350 degrees F. In a large bowl, combine cake mix, shortening, eggs, and water. Mix together until well blended. Roll into 1-inch balls and bake 9 minutes on an ungreased cookie sheet.

Prepare German Chocolate Frosting while cookies cool. Let frosting cool completely and then frost cookies. You can melt semi-sweet chocolate chips and drizzle over top of frosting if desired.

Makes 36 cookies.

GERMAN CHOCOLATE FROSTING

1   cup canned evaporated milk

1   cup granulated sugar

3   egg yolks, lightly beaten

½   cup margarine

1   teaspoon vanilla extract

1¾   cups flaked coconut

1¼   cups chopped pecans

Mix evaporated milk, sugar, egg yolks, margarine, and vanilla together in a medium saucepan. Stir constantly over medium heat until mixture comes to a slow boil. Cook, stirring constantly until mixture thickens, about 10 to 11 minutes. Remove from heat and stir in coconut and pecans. Cool frosting before spreading on cookies. Drizzle melted chocolate over frosted cookies if desired. This frosting recipe will also cover a 9x13-inch cake.

Slow Cooker Sweet and Sour Meatballs

Balsamic Asparagus

5-Minute Jell-O Salad

Slow Cooker Sweet and Sour Meatballs

Growing up, we cared more about the food than any big sports game going on. These meatballs are perfect for any game or party or for an easy and delicious meal.

1 **(10-ounce) jar sweet and sour sauce**	1 **medium red bell pepper, cubed**
¼ **cup light brown sugar**	1 **medium green bell pepper, cubed**
¼ **cup soy sauce**	1 **medium onion, cubed**
½ **teaspoon garlic powder**	1 **(20-ounce) can pineapple chunks, drained**
2 **pounds frozen meatballs**	

Spray inside of slow cooker with nonstick cooking spray. Place all ingredients inside the slow cooker and stir gently. Place lid on slow cooker. Cook on low 7 to 8 hours or on high 4 to 5 hours.

Serve over rice as a main dish or serve with toothpicks for a yummy appetizer.

Makes 8 servings.

Balsamic Asparagus

This is the perfect side dish to go with just about any meal. It only takes a few minutes to throw together, and it is absolutely delicious.

- 2 cups water
- 1 pound fresh asparagus, trimmed
- 2 tablespoons balsamic vinegar
- 1 tablespoon butter, melted
- ½ teaspoon minced garlic
- ¼ teaspoon salt
- ¼ teaspoon black pepper

In a large pan, bring water to a boil. Add asparagus, and boil, uncovered, 4 to 5 minutes or until tender. In a small bowl, whisk together vinegar, butter, garlic, salt, and pepper. Drain asparagus and drizzle with balsamic mixture.

Makes 4 servings.

5-Minute Jell-O Salad

Every Sunday my mom used to make a Jell-O salad. I grew up loving it (especially the green Jell-O with pineapple)! This is my favorite "fast" salad because you don't have to cook anything, it doesn't need to set up before you eat it, and it is *delicious!* —Kristen

1 (8-ounce) container low-fat nondairy whipped topping

1 (4-ounce) box strawberry Jell-O

1 (12-ounce) container fat-free cottage cheese

½ pound strawberries, sliced

1 banana, sliced

Whisk whipped topping and Jell-O in a large mixing bowl until well blended and most of the Jell-O is dissolved into the whipped topping. Fold in cottage cheese, strawberries, and bananas. Chill in refrigerator until ready to serve.

Makes 6 servings.

MENU 30

5-Star Grilled Chicken Teriyaki

Fresh Vegetables with Vegetable Dill Dip

Raspberry Lemonade Cupcakes

Vegetable Dill Dip

Some may argue that dip completely counteracts eating healthy vegetables, but a little of this flavorful dip goes a long way. Stick to a tablespoon or two and you will be just fine.

◇◇◇

1 cup mayonnaise	1 tablespoon dried parsley
1 cup sour cream	1 teaspoon seasoned salt
1 tablespoon dried dill weed	Sliced vegetables: carrots, broccoli, cauliflower, peppers, tomatoes, etc.
1 tablespoon dried minced onion	

Combine all ingredients together. Cover and store in fridge 4 to 6 hours before eating. (You can also make it the day before and allow the flavors to really meld together).

Serve with your favorite vegetables or crackers.

Makes 2 cups of dip—about 10 to 12 servings.

Raspberry Lemonade Cupcakes

For this recipe I took one of my favorite summer drinks and turned it into a cupcake. The end result was delicious! There are fresh raspberries in the batter and actual lemonade in the frosting, so you get a light, fresh taste that is perfect for summer. —Camille

CUPCAKES

1   (18.25-ounce) box white cake mix

1   (3.4-ounce) box vanilla instant pudding

3   tablespoons sweetened raspberry lemonade drink mix (such as Country Time Lemonade)

1   cup sour cream

2   teaspoons lemon zest

¾   cup water

¾   cup vegetable oil

4   egg whites

3   drops red food coloring

1   cup fresh raspberries

FROSTING

1   cup butter, softened

1   cup shortening

    Zest from 1 lemon

½   cup frozen raspberry lemonade concentrate, thawed

2   tablespoons milk

2   teaspoons vanilla extract

7½   cups powdered sugar

3 to 4   drops red food coloring

Preheat oven to 350 degrees F. Line 24 muffin tins with cupcake papers and set aside. In a large bowl, whisk together cake mix, pudding mix, and drink mix. Add sour cream, lemon zest, water, oil, and egg whites to the dry mix. Beat with electric mixer on medium speed about 2 minutes. Add drops of food coloring and mix in. Fold in raspberries and mix gently to incorporate.

Scoop batter into prepared muffin tins. Bake 15 to 20 minutes, until a toothpick inserted into one comes out clean. Allow to cool completely before frosting the cupcakes.

Prepare frosting by creaming butter, shortening, and lemon zest together. Add lemonade concentrate, milk, and vanilla and beat until smooth. Gradually add sugar, mixing well until light and fluffy. Beat in food coloring.

Pipe frosting onto the cupcakes. Place a fresh raspberry on top of each cupcake.

Makes 24 cupcakes.

5-Star Grilled Chicken Teriyaki

This recipe couldn't be any easier. Mix a couple of ingredients together in a bag, throw in some chicken, and let it soak all day long. Toss on the grill for dinner and you have a delicious meal that took only a couple of minutes to prep.

We call this 5-Star Chicken because the first time I made it, my husband took a bite and said, "Five stars. This chicken deserves five stars." I think you'll agree. —Camille

1   **pound boneless, skinless chicken breasts**

1   **cup teriyaki sauce**

¼   **cup lemon juice**

2   **cloves garlic, minced**

2   **teaspoons sesame oil**

Place chicken, teriyaki sauce, lemon juice, garlic, and sesame oil in a large resealable plastic bag. Close bag and shake to thoroughly coat the chicken. Place chicken in the refrigerator 8 to 12 hours, turning the bag once or twice throughout the day to make sure the chicken is marinating evenly.

When ready to cook, turn the grill on to high heat.

Remove chicken from bag and immediately throw away any remaining marinade. Grill 6 to 8 minutes on each side, or until juices run clear when chicken is pierced with a fork.

Makes 4 servings.

MEASUREMENT CONVERSION CHART

How many times when you are in the middle of cooking do you realize that the measuring spoon or cup that you need is in the dishwasher? This chart can help you quickly find what you need and remember all the different ways you can measure ingredients.

EQUIVALENT MEASUREMENTS

1 dash	$\frac{1}{16}$ teaspoon
1 pinch	$\frac{1}{8}$ teaspoon
3 teaspoons	1 tablespoon
$\frac{1}{8}$ cup	2 tablespoons
$\frac{1}{4}$ cup	4 tablespoons
$\frac{1}{3}$ cup	5 tablespoons + 1 teaspoon
$\frac{1}{2}$ cup	8 tablespoons
$\frac{2}{3}$ cup	10 tablespoons + 2 teaspoons
$\frac{3}{4}$ cup	12 tablespoons
1 cup	16 tablespoons
8 ounces	1 cup
2 cups	1 pint
2 pints	1 quart
4 quarts	1 gallon
16 ounces	1 pound

METRIC CONVERSIONS
Volume (mL = milliliter)

1 mL	$\frac{1}{4}$ teaspoon
2.5 mL	$\frac{1}{2}$ teaspoon
4 mL	$\frac{3}{4}$ teaspoon
5 mL	1 teaspoon
10 mL	2 teaspoons
15 mL	1 tablespoon
30 mL	2 tablespoons
59 mL	$\frac{1}{4}$ cup
79 mL	$\frac{1}{3}$ cup
118 mL	$\frac{1}{2}$ cup
178 mL	1 cup
473 mL	2 cups (1 pint)
.95 liter	4 cups (1 quart)
1 liter	1.06 quarts
3.8 liters	4 quarts (1 gallon)

WEIGHT

28 grams	1 ounce
113 grams	4 ounces
227 grams	8 ounces
454 grams	16 ounces (1 pound)

MENU 31

Oven-Baked Tacos

Zesty Guacamole

One-Bowl Chocolate Cake

Zesty Guacamole

I would eat guacamole for every meal if I could. Unfortunately, buying it at the store each week is expensive. I decided to make my own guacamole at home. Not only does it taste better, it's also cheaper! —Lauren

2 ripe avocados

1 small red onion, finely chopped

1 clove garlic, minced

1 ripe tomato, chopped

1 lime, juiced

Salt and pepper, to taste

Peel and mash avocados in a medium serving bowl. Stir in onion, garlic, tomato, and lime juice. Season with salt and pepper, to taste. Cover tightly with plastic wrap and chill 30 minutes to blend flavors.

Makes 6 servings.

Oven-Baked Tacos

If you're the mom of a picky eater who loves tacos but throws a fit when they break apart and the filling goes all over the place, these are for you. Baking the tacos softens the shell just a little bit and helps solidify the filling. The shells don't break into a million pieces and you can safely eat dinner without a single tear, which makes these oven-baked tacos a perfect 10 in my book! —Camille

1 medium onion, diced	1 cup chunky salsa
2 cloves garlic, minced	12 hard taco shells
1 pound lean ground beef	1½ cups shredded cheddar cheese
1 (1-ounce) packet taco seasoning	Optional toppings: diced tomatoes, lettuce, olives, sour cream
1 (15-ounce) can black beans, drained and rinsed	

Preheat oven to 400 degrees F. In a large skillet, heat oil over medium-high heat and add onion and garlic. Sauté about 5 minutes, until soft. Add beef and taco seasoning, cooking until meat is browned. Add beans and salsa. Mix well and reduce heat to let simmer a couple of minutes so flavors can meld and mixture can thicken.

In a 9x13-inch baking pan, line up all taco shells. Fill each one with a couple scoops of the beef mixture and pack down into the shell. Repeat until all the shells are filled. Top each taco with shredded cheese.

Bake 8 to 10 minutes, or until all the cheese is melted.

Serve with your favorite taco toppings (tomatoes, lettuce, olives, sour cream, guacamole, pico de gallo, hot sauce—whatever you like!).

Makes 4 to 6 servings.

One-Bowl Chocolate Cake

I love chocolate cake—especially when it's made from scratch. However, I hate doing dishes. Fortunately, this one-bowl recipe is here to save the day whenever I crave chocolate cake! —Camille

- 2 cups all-purpose flour
- 2 cups granulated sugar
- ½ cup cocoa powder
- 2 teaspoons baking soda
- 1 teaspoon baking powder
- ½ teaspoon salt
- 1 cup vegetable oil
- 1 cup buttermilk*
- 2 eggs
- 1 cup hot water
- Chocolate frosting
- Sprinkles (optional)

Preheat oven to 350 degrees F. Grease a 9x13-inch pan and set aside. In a large bowl, combine all dry ingredients. Mix in the oil, buttermilk, and eggs. Once the eggs are fully incorporated, pour in the hot water and mix well (batter will seem runny, but I promise it's okay).

Pour batter into prepared pan. Bake 33 to 38 minutes, until a toothpick inserted in the middle of the cake comes out clean. When the cake is completely cool, top with frosting and decorate with sprinkles.

*Don't have buttermilk? No worries! Simply make your own. Take 1 cup milk and add 1 tablespoon vinegar or lemon juice. Stir and let sit about 5 minutes. Use immediately.

Makes 20 servings.

Slow Cooker Sunday Dinner
Pot Roast

Mandarin Orange Pretzel Salad

White Chocolate Raspberry
Cheesecake

Mandarin Orange Pretzel Salad

Our mom brought this salad to many family parties. You can bet that when we get together as sisters now, one of us will bring this dish. It really is one of our favorites!

2 cups crushed pretzels	1 (8-ounce) container nondairy whipped topping
½ cup butter, melted	1 (6-ounce) box orange Jell-O
1 cup plus 3 tablespoons granulated sugar, divided	2 cups boiling water
1 (8-ounce) package cream cheese	1 (11-ounce) can mandarin oranges

Preheat oven to 350 degrees F. For the first layer, combine pretzels, melted butter, and 3 tablespoons sugar. Stir together until well blended. Press in 9x13-inch baking pan and bake 7 minutes. Cool completely.

For the second layer, beat 1 cup sugar and cream cheese together until smooth. Fold in whipped topping. Spread cream mixture over pretzel layer. Be sure to seal the cream cheese layer against the sides of the pan so that the Jell-O mixture will not be able to leak through when added.

For the third layer, mix Jell-O and boiling water until completely dissolved. Add oranges and let cool until slightly set. Pour over cream cheese layer and refrigerate until firm. Cut into squares and serve.

Makes about 12 servings.

Slow Cooker Sunday Dinner Pot Roast

Sunday dinner was always the best meal of the week growing up at our house, and pot roast was one of our staple Sunday meals. This is the easiest and yummiest pot roast recipe. You just can't mess it up!

- 2 tablespoons olive oil
- 2½ to 3 pounds beef chuck roast
- Salt and pepper
- 1 pound baby carrots
- 1 large sweet onion, diced
- 4 medium potatoes, cubed (red, Yukon gold, or russet)

- 4 cloves garlic, crushed
- 1 (16-ounce) can diced tomatoes (optional)
- 2 cups beef broth
- 1 chicken bouillon cube, dissolved in beef broth

Heat olive oil in a large sauté pan over medium-high heat. Pat beef with paper towels and season all sides generously with salt and pepper. Sear beef in the sauté pan until a nice crust forms, about 3 minutes on each side.

Place beef in slow cooker. Reserve drippings in pan and add carrots, onion, potatoes, and garlic, and sauté about 3 minutes. Pour in the diced tomatoes (with juices) and stir to combine. Arrange sautéed vegetables over beef and pour in beef broth and bouillon mixture.

Cook on low 7 to 8 hours.

Makes 6 to 8 servings.

POT ROAST GRAVY

- Pot Roast drippings/liquid
- 2 tablespoons butter, cold
- 2 tablespoons flour

- 1 teaspoon cornstarch (optional)
- 1 to 2 teaspoons cold water (optional)
- Freshly ground black pepper, to taste

Pour drippings out of the slow cooker into a small or medium saucepan. Simmer over medium-low heat about 5 minutes. Put butter and flour together in a small bowl and mash together with a fork until well combined. Slowly whisk the butter mixture into the drippings until it starts to thicken and combine.

For thick gravy, use the cornstarch as a thickening agent. Combine cornstarch with cold water until dissolved. Stir into gravy, whisking until smooth. Season with pepper.

White Chocolate Raspberry Cheesecake

If I could pick a favorite dessert it would be cheesecake. I can't get enough of the creamy texture of this cheesecake! —Kristen

1 (10-ounce) package frozen raspberries

½ cup plus 2 tablespoons granulated sugar, divided

2 teaspoons cornstarch

½ cup water

2 cups white chocolate chips

½ cup half-and-half

3 (8-ounce) packages cream cheese, softened

3 eggs

1 teaspoon vanilla extract

Pre-made or store-bought graham cracker pie crust

In a saucepan, combine raspberries, 2 tablespoons sugar, cornstarch, and water. Bring to boil, and continue boiling 5 minutes, or until sauce is thick. Strain sauce through a mesh strainer to remove seeds.

Preheat oven to 325 degrees F. In a pan over medium-low heat, melt white chocolate chips with half-and-half. Stir occasionally until smooth and set aside.

In a large bowl, mix together cream cheese and ½ cup sugar until smooth. Beat in eggs one at a time. Blend in vanilla and melted white chocolate. Pour half of batter over crust. Spoon 3 tablespoons raspberry sauce over batter. Pour remaining cheesecake batter into pan, and again spoon 3 tablespoons raspberry sauce over the top. Swirl batter with the tip of a knife to create a marbled effect.

Bake 55 to 60 minutes, or until filling is set. Cool, cover with plastic wrap, and refrigerate 8 hours before removing from pan. Serve with remaining raspberry sauce.

Makes 8 servings.

FAMILY PUMPKIN WALK

Every Halloween, our parents have a party for the grandkids. One year they thought it would be fun for the kids to bring their carved pumpkins to share.

Our family pumpkin walk tradition started out with just a few pumpkins in my parents' backyard but has now grown to a whole yard of pumpkins!

Our mom spends the whole day before the party carving pumpkins to show the kids. And once it is dark, we light candles in all of the pumpkins and let the kids walk around and admire them. They absolutely love it!

MENU 33

Oven-Fried Chicken

BBQ Macaroni Salad

Oatmeal Scotchies

BBQ Macaroni Salad

A summer barbecue isn't complete without a macaroni salad! This salad is full of flavor. The sauce gives it a kick to remember.

1 (16-ounce) box elbow macaroni

1 cup mayonnaise

½ cup barbecue sauce

⅛ teaspoon garlic powder

½ teaspoon chili powder

¼ teaspoon hot sauce

2 tablespoons apple cider vinegar

1 red bell pepper, seeded and finely chopped

1 rib celery, finely chopped

½ cup cubed cucumber

½ cup shredded carrots

2 tablespoons finely chopped green onions

4 tablespoons finely chopped purple onion

½ cup Colby Jack cheese, cubed

Cook macaroni according to package directions. Drain the noodles, rinse in cold water and drain again. In a large bowl, combine mayonnaise, barbecue sauce, seasonings, hot sauce, and vinegar. Add the drained noodles, chopped veggies, and cheese. Stir to combine and refrigerate before serving.

Makes 12 servings.

Oven-Fried Chicken

We don't have fried food at our home very often, but this oven-fried chicken tastes just as delicious as regular fried chicken, except without all the mess! —Elyse

◇◇

2 to 3	skinless, boneless chicken breasts, cut into strips
2	cups buttermilk
1	tablespoon seasoning salt

1	teaspoon black pepper
1	cup all-purpose flour
1	tablespoon paprika
½	cup butter

Put chicken strips and buttermilk in a large resealable plastic bag. Seal bag tightly and allow chicken to soak for at least an hour. Preheat oven to 400 degrees F. In a shallow pie pan, combine seasoning salt, pepper, flour, and paprika. Spray the bottom of a 9x13-inch baking pan with cooking spray. Cut up butter into pieces and place around the bottom of the pan. Place baking pan with butter in oven about 5 minutes, or until butter is melted and hot. Remove pan from oven.

Remove each piece of chicken from plastic bag and shake off excess buttermilk. Coat chicken pieces in seasoning mix. Place coated chicken pieces in the baking pan. Bake 15 minutes, remove pan from oven and turn each piece of chicken, then bake 15 more minutes, or until golden brown and cooked through.

Makes 2 to 3 servings.

Oatmeal Scotchies

My mom used to make these all the time when we were growing up, and the combination of oats and butterscotch chips is one of my favorites—and I am totally a chocolate chip cookie lover! I called my mom for the recipe, expecting it to be some secret family recipe, and I found out that she got it from the back of an oatmeal container years ago. So thank you, oatmeal container, for this amazing recipe! —Kendra

1¼ cups all-purpose flour

1 teaspoon baking soda

½ teaspoon salt

½ teaspoon ground cinnamon

1 cup butter or margarine, softened

¾ cup granulated sugar

¾ cup light brown sugar

2 large eggs

1 teaspoon vanilla extract or grated peel of 1 orange

3 cups quick or old-fashioned oats

1 package (about 2 cups) butterscotch chips

Preheat oven to 375 degrees F. Combine flour, baking soda, salt, and cinnamon in a small bowl. Beat butter, granulated sugar, brown sugar, eggs, and vanilla extract in a large mixer bowl. Gradually beat in flour mixture. Stir in oats and butterscotch chips. Drop by rounded tablespoon onto ungreased baking sheets.

Bake 7 to 8 minutes for chewy cookies or 9 to 10 minutes for crisp cookies. Cool on baking sheets 2 minutes; remove to wire racks to cool completely.

Makes 36 cookies.

MENU 34

Slow Cooker Pineapple BBQ Beef Sandwiches

Deviled Eggs

White Chocolate Chip Oatmeal Cookies

White Chocolate Chip Oatmeal Cookies

Whether you love cookie dough or baked cookies best, this recipe is for you!

◇◇

1 cup butter, softened	1 teaspoon baking powder
1 cup light brown sugar	1 teaspoon baking soda
1 cup granulated sugar	1 teaspoon salt
2 eggs	1½ cups rolled oats
2 teaspoons vanilla extract	2 cups white chocolate chips
3 cups all-purpose flour	

Preheat oven to 350 degrees F. In a bowl, beat together softened butter and sugars. Add in eggs and vanilla and mix well. Stir in flour, baking powder, baking soda, and salt until completely incorporated. Fold in oats and white chocolate chips. Drop by tablespoonfuls onto cookie sheets and bake 9 to 12 minutes. Remove from cookie sheets and let cool.

Makes about 5 dozen cookies.

Slow Cooker Pineapple BBQ Beef Sandwiches

The longer you let the beef cook, the better it becomes. The meat has a really yummy flavor and the pineapple adds just the right amount of sweetness. If you want to mix up your shredded beef sandwiches, give this recipe a try! —Elyse

1   (2- to 3-pound) beef rump roast

1   (20-ounce) can pineapple chunks, juice reserved

1   onion, diced

½   cup apple cider vinegar

⅓   cup light brown sugar

½   cup ketchup

1   tablespoon Dijon mustard

2   tablespoons Worcestershire sauce

Optional toppings: red onions, lettuce, tomatoes, provolone cheese

Spray slow cooker with cooking spray. Place roast inside.

In a separate bowl, mix together juice from pineapples, onion, vinegar, brown sugar, ketchup, mustard, and Worcestershire sauce. Pour over roast. Add pineapple chunks to roast and cook on low 10 hours or on high 5 to 6 hours. (I prefer the low-and-slow cooking method.)

When finished, shred meat using two forks. Serve meat on toasted buns, topped with your favorite sandwich fixings.

Makes 10 servings.

Deviled Eggs

I still remember the first time my husband made these deviled eggs—he kept telling me how easy they were and threw them together without even looking at a recipe. I was blown away (and fell in love with him even more)! Since then, I have made these eggs multiple times. They are such a quick and simple side dish that perfectly complements any summer meal! —Camille

6 **hard-boiled eggs**

Salt and pepper

2 **tablespoons mayonnaise**

1 **tablespoon yellow mustard**

2 **tablespoons dill pickle or sweet pickle relish**

Paprika

Peel shells off hard-boiled eggs and slice in half lengthwise. Using a spoon, gently remove yolks and place in a small bowl. Mash yolks into small pieces with a fork. Add mayonnaise, mustard, and relish to the yolks and mix until well combined and creamy.

Carefully scoop some yolk mixture into the hollow of each egg half. Repeat until all egg whites are filled. Lightly sprinkle with paprika and refrigerate until ready to serve.

Makes 6 servings.

Slow Cooker Philly Cheesesteak Sandwiches

Baked Seasoned Steak Fries

Fresh Fruit and Nutella Fruit Dip

Nutella Fruit Dip

I hate to admit it, but I can finish off a whole jar of Nutella by myself. I wanted to make something with Nutella, and this dip didn't disappoint! —Stephanie

½ cup Nutella

4 ounces fat-free cream cheese

½ cup nondairy whipped topping

In a large bowl, mix all ingredients together until smooth. Refrigerate until ready to serve. Serve with fresh fruit, graham crackers, brownie bites, etc.

Makes 1 cup.

Slow Cooker Philly Cheesesteak Sandwiches

This is one of my go-to easy meals! It is so simple to throw together and since it cooks all day, the meat is so tender it practically falls apart. My kids love to eat it on little rolls because it's the perfect size for their hands, but my husband eats his on a foot-long hoagie. —Camille

1½ **pounds beef round steak**	1 **package dry Italian dressing mix**
1 **green pepper, thinly sliced**	1 **large loaf French bread, sliced into sandwich lengths (or 4 to 6 hoagie buns)**
1 **medium onion, thinly sliced**	
1 **(14-ounce) can beef broth**	**Provolone cheese slices**

Spray slow cooker with cooking spray. Cut meat into strips, place in slow cooker. Add green pepper, onion, broth, and dressing mix. Cover and cook on low 7 to 8 hours, or on high 3 to 4 hours.

Spoon meat mixture onto bread, top with cheese. Another option is to toast bread in a 375 degree F. oven 5 to 10 minutes, add meat, cover with cheese, then bake an additional 5 minutes to melt the cheese.

My husband loves to top his sandwich with A.1. Steaksauce. Use any condiments you like!

Makes 4 to 6 servings (depending on size of hoagie rolls).

Baked Seasoned Steak Fries

I love going out to eat and getting a heaping serving of steak fries with my meal. To save myself a few calories, I decided to try a baked version at home! —Stephanie

4 large russet potatoes, peeled and sliced into thin wedges	2 teaspoons garlic powder
¼ cup olive oil	2 teaspoons chili powder
2 teaspoons paprika	2 teaspoons onion powder

Preheat oven to 450 degrees F. Place wedges in sealable plastic bag. In a large mixing bowl, whisk together olive oil, paprika, garlic powder, chili powder, and onion powder. Add mixture to bag and toss until evenly coated. Cover a baking sheet in foil and spread coated potato wedges onto it. Bake 40 to 45 minutes, or until golden and cooked through.

Makes 6 to 8 servings.

Deep Dish Pizza

Baked Buffalo Wings

Wedge Salad

Wedge Salad

This salad is so delicious! The blue cheese dressing is full of flavor and makes this salad a family favorite.

SALAD

1 head iceberg lettuce, cut into 4 wedges	12 slices cooked bacon, crumbled
2 cups grape tomatoes, cut into halves	1 cup blue cheese, crumbled
1 cup chopped red onion	1 cup pecan pieces, toasted

DRESSING

1½ cups mayonnaise	½ teaspoon garlic powder
1½ cups buttermilk	½ teaspoon onion powder
1 cup blue cheese, crumbled	½ teaspoon black pepper

Place each lettuce wedge on a plate. Top with grape tomato halves and onion. Sprinkle on crumbled bacon, blue cheese, and toasted pecan pieces. Mix together all dressing ingredients and drizzle on top of salad.

Makes 4 servings.

Deep Dish Pizza

Why order out for pizza when you can make it at home? It's simple, easy, and always a big hit with kids.

◇◇

PIZZA DOUGH

1⅓ cup warm water (105 degrees F.)

¼ cup nonfat dry milk

½ teaspoon salt

4 cups all-purpose flour

1 tablespoon granulated sugar

1 (¼-ounce) package dry yeast

2 tablespoons vegetable oil

SAUCE

1 (8-ounce) can tomato sauce

1 teaspoon dry oregano

½ teaspoon marjoram

½ teaspoon dry basil

½ teaspoon garlic salt

TOPPINGS

2 to 3 cups shredded mozzarella cheese

Your family's favorite toppings: pepperoni, sausage, bell peppers, onions, etc.

FOR DOUGH:

Put yeast, sugar, salt, and dry milk in a large bowl. Add water and stir to mix well. Allow to sit for two minutes. Add oil and stir again. Add flour and stir until dough forms and flour is absorbed.

Turn out onto a flat surface and knead about 10 minutes. Divide dough into three balls. Put 3 tablespoons oil in three 9-inch cake pans, making sure it spreads evenly. Using a rolling pin, roll out each dough ball to about a 9-inch circle. Place in cake pans.

Spray the outer edge of dough with cooking spray. Cover with a plate. Place in warm area and allow to rise 1 to 1½ hours.

FOR SAUCE:

Preheat oven to 475 degrees F. Combine tomato sauce, oregano, marjoram, basil, and garlic salt.

Spoon ⅓ cup sauce onto dough and spread to within 1 inch of edge. Distribute ¼ cup shredded mozzarella cheese on sauce. Place toppings of your choice in this order: pepperoni or ham, vegetables, other meats (cooked ground sausage or beef). Top with remaining mozzarella cheese. Bake 10 to 15 minutes, or until cheese is bubbling and outer crust is brown.

Makes three 9-inch pizzas.

Baked Buffalo Wings

If you are looking for a yummy appetizer, look no further. These wings are so simple to make—and no one will know they are baked instead of fried!

- ¾ cup all-purpose flour
- ½ teaspoon cayenne pepper
- ½ teaspoon garlic powder
- ½ teaspoon salt
- 20 chicken wings

- ½ cup butter, melted
- ½ cup hot pepper sauce (for example, Frank's RedHot sauce)
- Ranch dressing or blue cheese dressing, for dipping

Line a baking sheet with aluminum foil and lightly grease with cooking spray. Place flour, cayenne pepper, garlic powder, and salt into a resealable plastic bag and shake to mix. Make sure chicken wings are completely dry and add them to the bag. Seal bag and toss until wings are well coated with flour mixture.

Place wings onto prepared baking sheet and place in refrigerator. Chill at least 1 hour to prevent wings from getting soggy. (For faster preparation, place wings in the freezer about 20 minutes.)

Preheat oven to 400 degrees F.

Whisk together melted butter and hot sauce in a small bowl. Dip wings into butter mixture, and place back on baking sheet. Bake about 45 minutes, until chicken is no longer pink in the center and is crispy on the outside. The internal temperature should reach 165 degrees F. Rotate wings halfway through cooking time so they cook evenly.

Serve with your favorite dips or eat plain—they are delicious either way!

Makes 20 wings.

DINNER ON THE DOORSTEP

Every year on Christmas Eve, we select one family in need and leave the ingredients for an entire Christmas dinner on their doorstep.

When we were little, we all loved to help pack the boxes full of food and extra gifts we had picked out for the kids. We loved the feeling we had as we drove silently to a neighbor's house to drop off dinner on the doorstep. There was always a debate to see which sister got to help take the packages to the front door and which sister got to ring the doorbell and run like crazy back to the car without being caught.

After ringing and running, we would wait for a few minutes and then drive by the house casually, just to make sure the family found our surprise.

Providing service as a family to another family made us feel so grateful for everything we had, and it always brought us closer together. Plus we created memories we would never forget—like the time we knocked and the door flew wide open or when Elyse tripped on the way back to the car.

But most importantly, this tradition instilled in us the importance of giving freely to others.

We always did this activity at Christmastime, but service can be done year round. Here are some other dinner ideas:

Easter: Deli meat and buns for sandwiches, fresh fruit, cookies.

Fourth of July: Hamburger patties and buns, a bag of chips, a container of potato salad, condiments (ketchup, mustard, relish), a dozen cupcakes.

Halloween: Chicken noodle soup, a bag of rolls, a pumpkin pie.

Christmas: A turkey or ham, a bag of rolls, a box of stuffing mix, a bowl of mashed potatoes, the fixings for green bean casserole, a container of gravy, a pie or a carton of ice cream.

WHAT YOU'LL NEED

- **The fixings for a complete dinner**
- **A giving heart**
- **A willing runner**
- **A fast getaway car**

MENU
37

Homemade Bread Bowls

Creamy Chicken Chili

Slow Cooker Rocky Road Chocolate Fondue

Homemade Bread Bowls

Nothing goes better with soup than a nice, warm bread bowl. These are so easy, I will never buy them from the bakery again! —Elyse

2 cups plus 4 tablespoons warm water	2 tablespoons granulated sugar
2 packages of active dry yeast (5½ teaspoons)	3 teaspoons salt
½ cup butter, melted	6½ cups all-purpose flour

Pour warm water into a stand mixer or large mixing bowl; sprinkle in yeast. Let dissolve a few minutes, until yeast becomes foamy. Add melted butter, sugar, and salt and mix until combined. Gradually add flour. Once combined, allow mixer to knead the dough about 5 minutes. (You can do this by hand instead of using a mixer, but it may get a little tiring!)

Preheat oven to 425 degrees F. Punch dough down and form into 6 balls of equal size. Place on a greased cookie sheet and let rise until doubled. Bake 20 to 25 minutes, or until golden brown. Let cool and cut off the top, remove some of the bread from the inside and fill with soup or dip.

Makes 6 bread bowls.

Creamy Chicken Chili

This chili is thick and has a little kick to it. It is easy to make and oh-so-delicious.

1   pound boneless, skinless chicken breast cut into ½-inch cubes

1   medium onion, chopped

1½ teaspoons garlic powder

1   tablespoon vegetable oil

2   (15-ounce) cans small white beans, rinsed and drained

1   (14-ounce) can chicken broth

2   (4-ounce) cans chopped green chilies

1   teaspoon salt

1   teaspoon ground cumin

1   teaspoon dried oregano

½   teaspoon black pepper

    Big pinch of cayenne pepper

1   cup sour cream

½   cup heavy whipping cream

In a large pan, sauté chicken, onion, and garlic powder in oil until chicken is no longer pink. Add beans, broth, chilies, and seasonings. Bring to a boil. Reduce heat to low and simmer uncovered 30 minutes. Remove from heat. Stir in sour cream and whipping cream. Serve immediately.

Makes 7 servings.

Slow Cooker Rocky Road Chocolate Fondue

We use our slow cookers for a lot of dinners, but did you ever think to use them for dessert? My kids love finding new things to dip into this warm chocolate and it is so fun to munch on while we watch a family show. This would also be the perfect dessert for a romantic date night. —Camille

1½ tablespoons butter	1½ cups miniature marshmallows
2 (4.25-ounce) Hershey's Chocolate with Almonds candy bars	3 tablespoons milk
	½ cup heavy whipping cream

Place butter, chocolate, marshmallows, and milk in a 1- to 2-quart slow cooker that has been sprayed with cooking spray. Cover and cook on low heat 1½ hours, stirring every 30 minutes until melted and smooth. Gradually stir in whipping cream. Cover and keep warm for serving, up to 2 hours.

Serve with bite-sized brownie pieces, bananas, apples, marshmallows, graham crackers, strawberries, cinnamon bears, cookies, mandarin oranges, or anything else you like. I like to use wooden skewers or large toothpicks to pick up the bite-sized food and dip it in the chocolate.

Makes 6 to 8 servings.

Marinated Steak Shish Kebabs

Ranch Roasted Potatoes

Layered Peanut Butter Brownies

Ranch Roasted Potatoes

These potatoes are a family favorite because they are so easy to prepare and use ingredients commonly found in the pantry.

2 pounds red potatoes, washed and quartered

¼ cup vegetable or olive oil

1 (1-ounce) packet dry Ranch dressing mix

Preheat oven to 450 degrees F. Cover a baking sheet with foil and set aside. Place potatoes in a resealable plastic bag and add oil. Toss to coat completely and add dry salad dressing mix to the bag. Toss once again to coat potatoes in dressing mix. Bake on prepared baking sheet 35 minutes, or until potatoes are brown and crisp.

Makes 6 servings.

Marinated Steak Shish Kebabs

This recipe is so simple and delicious it can make anyone feel like a fabulous chef. If you plan to use wooden skewers for the kebabs, soak the skewers in water for at least 30 minutes before threading with meat and veggies.

MARINADE

1 cup soy sauce	2 tablespoons vegetable oil
½ cup white vinegar	2 teaspoons minced garlic
½ cup brown sugar	1 teaspoon ground ginger
¼ cup diced onion	Salt and pepper, to taste

KEBABS

1 to 2 pounds sirloin or flank steak, cut into 1-inch cubes

1 red onion, cut into chunks

1 green bell pepper, cut into chunks

Mushrooms

Whisk all marinade ingredients together in a bowl or container. Place pieces of steak in marinade and pierce with a fork to allow juices to soak into meat. Cover and store in refrigerator at least 3 hours (the longer the better). After meat has marinated, slide alternating pieces of meat, onion, bell pepper, and mushrooms onto skewers. Heat grill to medium-high heat and grill kebabs 8 to 10 minutes, or until done.

Makes 4 to 6 servings.

Layered Peanut Butter Brownies

These brownies are so good, you could easily devour a whole pan by yourself. But you'll make more friends if you are willing to share. ☺

1	cup unsalted butter, softened	1½	cups all-purpose flour
⅓	cup cocoa powder	1	teaspoon salt
2	cups granulated sugar	2	teaspoons vanilla extract
4	eggs	1	(18-ounce) jar creamy peanut butter

FROSTING

⅓	cup milk	10	large marshmallows
¼	cup cocoa powder	2	cups powdered sugar
½	cup unsalted butter		

Preheat oven to 350 degrees F. Grease a 10x15-inch baking sheet and set aside.

In a large bowl, cream together butter, cocoa, and sugar with an electric mixer until smooth. Add eggs one at a time, mixing after each addition. Carefully add flour, salt, and vanilla and mix well. Spread brownie batter on prepared baking sheet. Bake 22 to 25 minutes and let cool for a few minutes.

While brownies cool, melt peanut butter in the microwave on high power in 60-second increments, stirring after each cycle, until smooth. Spread peanut butter over warm brownies and refrigerate until peanut butter has firmed up, about 30 minutes.

Make the frosting by combining milk, cocoa, butter, and marshmallows in a medium saucepan. Cook over medium heat, stirring until marshmallows are melted and mixture is smooth. Remove from heat and carefully mix in powdered sugar. Once frosting is smooth, spread over peanut butter layer and place brownies back in the refrigerator for 30 minutes, until set.

Makes 3 to 4 dozen brownies (depending on how big you cut them).

Slow Cooker Cranberry
Pork Loin

Brown Sugar and Bacon
Green Beans

5-Minute Creamy Key Lime Pie

Slow Cooker Cranberry Pork Loin

This recipe is definitely a crowd pleaser. The meat is so tender and juicy, you won't even need a knife!

- 3 pounds boneless pork loin or tenderloin
- 1 (16-ounce) can whole cranberry sauce
- ¼ cup Worcestershire sauce
- 1 tablespoon light brown sugar
- 1 teaspoon yellow mustard

Place roast in a slow cooker coated with cooking spray. Combine the rest of the ingredients and pour over roast. Cook on high 4 to 5 hours or on low 6 to 8 hours, making sure that its internal temperature reaches 145 degrees F. Remove roast, slice, and serve.

To make a gravy, simply add a little water and cornstarch mixture to the juices left in the slow cooker and whisk until combined.

Makes 6 to 8 servings.

Brown Sugar and Bacon Green Beans

The sweet from the brown sugar and the salty from the bacon make these beans taste pretty much like candy. Add a good amount of butter and you have an *incredible* dish!

1 (16-ounce) package frozen green beans

6 strips bacon, cooked and cut into 1-inch pieces

¼ cup butter

¼ cup light brown sugar

Garlic salt, to taste

In a large skillet, fry the bacon over medium heat until done but not quite crisp. Drain off grease and add butter and brown sugar. Cook, stirring occasionally, over medium heat until sugar has dissolved.

Place green beans in a pot and fill with about 1 inch of water. Bring water to a boil and place lid on the pot. Steam beans over medium heat until cooked through, about 5 to 8 minutes. Drain water from beans, season with garlic salt, and stir in sugar and bacon mixture. Serve immediately.

If sugar mixture starts to harden, quickly reheat it before pouring over beans.

Makes 4 servings.

5-Minute Creamy Key Lime Pie

I found this recipe on the back of a pre-made graham cracker crust package. This creamy pie seriously only takes 5 minutes to throw together—time yourself! —Stephanie

¼ cup water

1 (.3-ounce) package sugar-free lime Jell-O

2 (6-ounce) containers Key lime pie yogurt

1 (8-ounce) tub frozen nondairy whipped topping, thawed

1 pre-made graham cracker crust

In a microwave-safe measuring cup, heat water 45 to 90 seconds or until boiling. Whisk in Jell-O until dissolved.

In a large bowl, whisk together Jell-O mixture and yogurt. Fold in whipped topping. Carefully spread in crust. Refrigerate at least 4 hours or until set. Garnish with whipped cream or sliced limes, as desired.

Makes 8 servings.

Baked Crispy Chicken Parmesan

Mini Garlic Monkey Bread

Snickerdoodle Blondies

Mini Garlic Monkey Bread

I love a hot, buttery piece of garlic bread with my pasta. This is a simple side dish that will go perfectly with your Italian-inspired meal. —Elyse

2	(7.5-ounce) cans buttermilk biscuits	2	tablespoons dried parsley
6	tablespoons butter, melted	¼	cup grated Parmesan cheese, plus more for garnishing
4	cloves garlic, minced		

Preheat oven to 400 degrees F. Lightly grease a 12-cup muffin tin with cooking spray.

Cut each biscuit into quarters and place in a bowl. Combine butter, garlic, parsley, and ¼ cup Parmesan cheese. Pour over biscuit pieces. Gently toss together until everything is evenly coated with the butter mixture.

Place 4 to 5 biscuit pieces in each muffin cup. Sprinkle with additional Parmesan cheese. Bake 12 to 14 minutes, or until golden. Serve warm.

Makes 12 servings.

Baked Crispy Chicken Parmesan

My husband and I have been trying to eat healthier, so this baked version of Chicken Parmesan was right up our alley. My husband would never have known the chicken wasn't fried if I hadn't told him! —Elyse

2   cups Pepperidge Farm® Four Cheese and Garlic Croutons

4   boneless, skinless chicken breasts

1   egg, beaten

1   cup marinara sauce, heated

¼   cup shredded mozzarella cheese

Preheat oven to 375 degrees F. Spray baking sheet with vegetable cooking spray. Place croutons in resealable plastic bag, pressing most of the air out. Close and crush with rolling pin to form crumbs.

Dip chicken into egg. Coat with crumbs. Place chicken on prepared baking sheet. Spray chicken with vegetable cooking spray. Bake 20 to 30 minutes, or until internal temperature reaches 165 degrees F. Spoon heated marinara sauce over chicken and sprinkle with cheese.

Makes 4 servings.

Snickerdoodle Blondies

One of my favorite memories is coming home from school to a house smelling like Snickerdoodles. I don't mind making cookies but sometimes I don't have the time to roll out every single one and make multiple batches. These Snickerdoodle Blondies are so easy and delicious! —Kendra

1	cup salted butter, room temperature
2	eggs
2	cups light brown sugar

1	tablespoon vanilla extract
2⅔	cups all-purpose flour
2	teaspoons baking powder

CINNAMON TOPPING

2	tablespoons granulated sugar
2	teaspoons ground cinnamon

Preheat oven to 350 degrees F. Combine butter, eggs, brown sugar, and vanilla. Combine flour and baking powder in separate bowl and stir into egg mixture. Spread in a greased 9x13-inch dish. The batter will be thick, almost like a cookie mixture. Combine cinnamon topping ingredients and sprinkle over top. Bake 25 to 30 minutes, or until top springs back when pressed. Once it cools, it will harden more.

Makes 12 bars.

MENU 41

Slow Cooker Herbed
Turkey Breast

Loaded Baked Sweet Potatoes

Baked Pumpkin Spice
Doughnut Holes

Slow Cooker Herbed Turkey Breast

You don't need to wait for Thanksgiving to make a turkey! With some turkey breasts, seasonings, and your slow cooker, you can have Thanksgiving-worthy turkey any day of the week. —Camille

1 (6- to 9-pound) boneless turkey breast	1 tablespoon onion powder
1 onion, diced	1 tablespoon dried parsley
¾ cup water	1 tablespoon seasoned salt
1 (1-ounce) packet dry onion soup mix	1 tablespoon dried oregano
2 tablespoons garlic powder	1 tablespoon dried basil

Spray slow cooker with cooking spray and place turkey and diced onion inside. In a small bowl, mix together water and onion soup mix and spread evenly over turkey.

In another small bowl, mix together remaining ingredients and sprinkle over turkey breast.

Cook on low 8 to 9 hours, or until turkey is very tender and the seasonings have flavored the meat. Insert meat thermometer into the thickest part of the breast and make sure it reads at least 165 degrees F. to ensure turkey is fully cooked.

Makes 8 to 10 servings.

Loaded Baked Sweet Potatoes

I can honestly say that my favorite dish each Thanksgiving is the sweet potatoes. I think this twist on the sweet potato may possibly be my new favorite way to eat them! —Kristen

3 to 5	medium sweet potatoes	⅛	teaspoon pure vanilla extract
1	tablespoon melted butter		Pinch cinnamon
1	tablespoon dark brown sugar		Mini marshmallows

Preheat oven to 400 degrees F. Rinse each sweet potato, scrub clean, pat dry, and poke holes all over with fork. Line baking sheet with foil. Place potatoes on the baking sheet and bake 45 to 50 minutes, or until soft.

While potatoes are baking, combine melted butter, brown sugar, cinnamon, and vanilla in a small mixing bowl.

After removing potatoes from the oven, carefully slice an opening into each, lengthwise. Fill the open gap of each potato with a handful of mini marshmallows. Pour butter-sugar mixture evenly over potatoes. Top with another handful of mini marshmallows.

Heat broiler. Place baking pan with sweet potatoes under broiler 30 seconds, or until marshmallows are golden brown. Keep an eye on them so they don't burn. Sprinkle potatoes with a pinch of cinnamon and serve.

Makes 3 to 5 servings.

Baked Pumpkin Spice Doughnut Holes

I love that these doughnuts are baked instead of fried. They taste amazing and literally melt in your mouth.
—Kristen

◇◇◇◇◇◇◇◇◇◇◇◇◇◇◇◇◇◇◇◇◇◇◇◇◇◇◇◇◇◇◇◇◇◇

1¾ cups all-purpose flour

2 teaspoons baking powder

½ teaspoon salt

½ teaspoon cinnamon

½ teaspoon nutmeg

½ teaspoon allspice

⅛ teaspoon ground cloves

⅓ cup vegetable oil

½ cup brown sugar

1 egg

1 teaspoon vanilla extract

¾ cup canned plain pumpkin (not pumpkin pie filling)

½ cup milk

COATING

2 tablespoons butter, melted

⅓ cup granulated sugar

1 tablespoon cinnamon

Preheat oven to 350 degrees F. Spray a 24-cup mini muffin tin with cooking spray. In a medium bowl, whisk together flour, baking powder, salt, cinnamon, nutmeg, allspice, and cloves.

In a large bowl, whisk together oil, brown sugar, egg, vanilla, pumpkin, and milk, until smooth. Add dry ingredients and mix until just combined. Do not over-mix! Divide batter evenly among muffin cups. Bake 10 to 12 minutes or until a toothpick comes out clean.

While doughnuts bake, melt butter in one bowl and combine granulated sugar and cinnamon in another bowl. Remove doughnuts from oven and cool until just cool enough to handle. Dip each doughnut in melted butter and roll in cinnamon sugar to coat. Delicious served warm or at room temperature.

Makes 24 doughnuts.

DIY AT-HOME FAMILY RESTAURANT

Many years ago, on Valentine's Day, it was getting close to dinnertime and Mom was nowhere to be found. A few of us started searching for her and discovered the door to the toy room was closed. As we got closer, we found a sign on the door that read: "Family Restaurant—Please wait to be seated."

Excited, we gathered up all the sisters and Dad and patiently waited for Mom to let us in. When the door finally opened, we saw that our toy room had been transformed into a makeshift restaurant. There was a large quilt on the floor, set up like a picnic blanket, with place settings for each of us. At each place setting was a homemade menu with the specials of the day: pizza, breadsticks, and salad.

Mom took our orders then returned with all our drinks and food. It may have just been take-out food, but the setting was what made the whole night memorable. We loved being able to sit on the floor, in a room that we had never eaten in before. The memory of this night has remained with me. —Camille

WHAT YOU'LL NEED

- Let your kids help with the fun and assign them jobs in the "restaurant": maître d', waiter/waitress, busboy, etc.

- Every restaurant needs an awesome name! Let your kids brainstorm ideas and pick the one you all like the best. Make signs to put on the door or in the restaurant.

- Make a menu. You could do something simple like we did (take-out pizza), or you could put together some of your kids' favorite meal options. Let your kids illustrate the menu or cut pictures out of magazines of what each menu item looks like.

- Consider a theme night for your dinner:

  - Finger Foods (all foods must be eaten with your hands)

  - Backwards Dinner (eat dessert first)

  - Hawaiian Night (wear leis, eat Hawaiian haystacks and pineapple)

  - Tea Party (serve small tea sandwiches, drink out of teacups)

  - Italian Night (spaghetti, breadsticks, and spumoni for dessert)

  - Movie Night (watch *Cloudy with a Chance of Meatballs* and eat meatball sandwiches)

- Turn it into a math lesson and add prices to each item on the menu. Have your child calculate the cost of the bill, plus tax and tip.

Parmesan-Crusted Tilapia

Asparagus with Maple Mustard Glaze

Take 5 Cake Mix Bars

Asparagus with Maple Mustard Glaze

I tend to get a little bit lazy in preparing vegetables. My husband recently informed me that he can't handle any more bags of steamed veggies, so I made this delicious alternative. —Elyse

2 pounds asparagus	2 tablespoons Dijon mustard
2 tablespoons real maple syrup (maple-flavor syrup or honey can be substituted)	2 tablespoons olive oil

Snap off tough ends of asparagus spears. In 12-inch skillet or 4-quart Dutch oven, heat 1 inch of water (salted, if desired) to boiling. Add asparagus. Return to boil; reduce heat to medium. Cover and cook 4 to 5 minutes, or until asparagus is crisp-tender; drain. In a small bowl, mix maple syrup, mustard, and oil. Drizzle over asparagus and serve immediately.

Makes 4 to 6 servings.

Parmesan-Crusted Tilapia

This tilapia tastes amazing *and* it's good for you!

◇◇◇

4 tilapia fillets	1 teaspoon garlic powder
¼ cup crushed Ritz crackers	3 tablespoons lemon juice
¼ cup grated Parmesan cheese	Salt and pepper, to taste
1 tablespoon Italian seasoning	Olive oil

Preheat oven to 425 degrees F. Thaw and rinse tilapia fillets if frozen. Pat dry. Combine crackers, Parmesan, Italian seasoning, and garlic powder in a small bowl and mix well.

Pour 1 tablespoon of lemon juice on a plate. Place a fillet in lemon juice, sprinkle with desired amount of salt and black pepper. Turn fillet over in lemon juice and sprinkle seasoning on other side. Place fillet in Parmesan mixture, patting it all over to coat. Put covered fillets in a foil-lined 9x13-inch pan. Sprinkle a little lemon juice over fillets and drizzle or spray them lightly with olive oil.

Bake about 20 minutes or until fillets easily flake with a fork and edges are browning. If desired, sprinkle additional Parmesan on top.

Makes 4 servings.

Take 5 Cake Mix Bars

Take 5 is one of my favorite candy bars. I love the combination of the salty pretzels and peanut butter mixed with the sweetness of milk chocolate and caramel. It doesn't get much better than that—unless you add a little cake mix! —Elyse

1 (15.25-ounce) box yellow cake mix	⅓ cup plus ¼ cup creamy peanut butter
2 eggs, divided	4 ounces cream cheese, softened
⅓ cup butter, softened	1 cup powdered sugar
2 tablespoons milk	1¼ cups caramel candies, cut in half
⅔ cup crushed pretzels	1 cup milk chocolate chips

Preheat oven to 350 degrees F. In a large bowl, combine cake mix, 1 egg, butter, and milk until it forms a thick batter. Divide batter in half. Mix crushed pretzels in one half of batter. Press batter with pretzels into a greased 9x13-inch pan. Bake 8 to 9 minutes, or until batter is barely set.

In a separate bowl, cream together 1 egg, peanut butter, cream cheese, and powdered sugar until smooth. Carefully spread peanut butter mixture over partially baked pretzel batter. Sprinkle halved caramel squares and chocolate chips over peanut butter layer. Pour remaining cake batter over bars.

Bake 18 to 20 minutes, until cake batter on top is golden and puffy. Let cool and serve.

Makes 16 bars.

Fall-off-the-Bone BBQ Ribs

Cornbread Muffins

Twix Caramel Popcorn

Cornbread Muffins

Nothing goes better with barbecue than cornbread! These muffins are soft and are the perfect size for little hands.

1 cup all-purpose flour	⅓ cup granulated sugar
1 cup cornmeal	1 egg
1 teaspoon salt	1¼ cups milk
4 teaspoons baking powder	3 tablespoons butter, melted

Preheat oven to 350 degrees F. Combine ingredients in a large bowl, mixing 1 minute using a hand beater. Pour batter into a 12-cup muffin tin sprayed with nonstick cooking spray. Bake 15 to 20 minutes or until golden brown.

Makes 12 muffins.

Fall-off-the-Bone BBQ Ribs

These ribs will make everyone think that you slaved all day, but it couldn't be any easier. The ribs literally fall apart from slow cooking all day. Even though they are fully cooked before grilling, this last step is the icing on the cake—the barbecue sauce turns to a sticky glaze, and they are incredibly delicious. (Warning: You will need *a lot* of napkins to clean your hands off when you are done!) —Elyse

1   (2 to 3-pound) rack of ribs (I use pork loin ribs)

3½   cups pineapple juice, divided

1½   cups light brown sugar

1   (16-ounce) bottle barbecue sauce (I love Famous Dave's Rich and Sassy sauce)

Spray the slow cooker with cooking spray (or use a slow cooker liner). Cut slab of ribs into individual-serving sections (about 2 to 3 ribs each). Place ribs into slow cooker.

Mix 3¼ cups pineapple juice and brown sugar together and pour over ribs. Cook on high 7 to 8 hours or on low 10 to 12 hours. Ribs should reach an internal temperature of 145 degrees F.

When finished, use tongs to gently pull them out (they will literally fall apart when you touch them) and set aside. Turn grill to medium heat. Mix together bottle of barbecue sauce and ¼ cup pineapple juice.

Place ribs gently on the grill and brush with barbecue sauce. Turn ribs twice, slathering with more sauce each time. They will take about 10 to 15 minutes to glaze over. As soon as sauce starts to turn sticky, they are done!

Serve immediately and enjoy!

Makes 4 servings.

Twix Caramel Popcorn

This popcorn is the perfect snack for a movie night or a party! It's a perfect mix of sweet and crunchy and so easy to make. But we have to warn you . . . it can be very addicting!

- 5 quarts plain air-popped popcorn (equals about 1 cup popcorn kernels)
- 1 cup butter
- 2 cups light brown sugar
- ½ cup light corn syrup
- 1 teaspoon salt
- ½ teaspoon baking soda
- 1 teaspoon vanilla extract
- 24 Fun Size Twix candy bars, chopped into bite-sized pieces
- 2 cups milk chocolate chips, melted

Preheat oven to 250 degrees F. Place the popped corn in a large bowl. Set bowl aside.

In a deep (preferably heavy-bottom) saucepan, melt butter over medium heat. Stir in brown sugar, corn syrup, and salt. Bring to a boil, stirring constantly. Let mixture boil about 4 minutes without stirring. Remove saucepan from heat and mix in baking soda and vanilla extract. Pour caramel over popcorn in the bowl and gently stir until all of the popcorn is covered.

Spread popcorn on two large ungreased cookie sheets and bake about an hour, stirring every 15 minutes. Remove popcorn from oven and, while warm, break into pieces.

Mix in chopped candy bars. Drizzle melted chocolate chips over the popcorn. Let popcorn cool until the chocolate hardens, about 30 minutes. Store at room temperature in an airtight container.

Makes 12 servings.

Avocado Chicken Enchiladas

Fresh Lime Salsa

Tres Leches Cake

Fresh Lime Salsa

This salsa is so fresh and good that I could literally eat it by the spoonful. The fresh lime juice really takes it over the top! —Lauren

6 Roma tomatoes, diced	1 (15.25-ounce) can white corn, drained
2 avocados, diced	¼ cup fresh cilantro, finely chopped
1 medium red onion, finely diced	¼ cup fresh lime juice (about 2 limes)
1 (15.25-ounce) can black beans, drained and rinsed	2 tablespoons white vinegar

Combine all ingredients in a large bowl and serve with chips. Also delicious with grilled chicken!

(I recommend making this a couple of hours before serving so that all the flavors can meld together.)

Makes 8 servings.

Avocado Chicken Enchiladas

My favorite part of these enchiladas is how the homemade sauce cooks into the tortillas. These are delicious and a must-try! —Kristen

ENCHILADA SAUCE

- 3 garlic cloves, minced
- 1 tablespoon butter
- 1 tablespoon all-purpose flour
- 1 cup chicken or vegetable stock
- 2 teaspoons cumin
- ¼ teaspoon salt
- ¼ teaspoon freshly ground black pepper
- ½ cup fat-free sour cream
- 1 cup mild or medium salsa verde
- ½ cup chopped cilantro

ENCHILADAS

- 3 to 4 cups cooked chicken breasts, chopped or shredded
- 2 cups shredded Mexican blend cheese, divided
- 3 avocados, peeled and chopped
- 8 flour tortillas

Preheat oven to 375 degrees F. In medium saucepan, sauté garlic in butter about 1 minute on medium-high heat. Stir in flour and cook about 2 more minutes. Stir in broth, cumin, salt, and pepper, and bring to a simmer. Remove from heat and stir in sour cream, salsa verde, and cilantro, until smooth.

Prepare a 9x13-inch baking dish with cooking spray. Add about ½ cup sauce to the pan and spread until bottom of dish is evenly coated.

Lay out a tortilla and add chicken, shredded cheese, and avocado to one end of the tortilla and roll. Place the rolled tortilla seam-side down and repeat until the pan is full.

Pour the remaining sauce over the enchiladas. Cover with 1 cup of cheese and bake about 20 minutes, or until cheese is bubbling.

Makes 8 servings.

Tres Leches Cake

My husband spent some time in Uruguay and he was the one who introduced me to tres leches cake. If you have never tried it, I highly recommend it! —Kristen

CAKE

1 cup all-purpose flour	1 cup granulated sugar
1 teaspoon baking powder	5 eggs
½ teaspoon salt	1½ teaspoons vanilla extract
8 tablespoons unsalted butter, room temperature	

GLAZE

1 (12-ounce) can evaporated milk	1 cup half-and-half
1 (14-ounce) can sweetened condensed milk	

TOPPING

2 cups heavy whipping cream	1 teaspoon vanilla extract
½ cup granulated sugar	

Preheat the oven to 350 degrees F. Spray a 9x13-inch pan with cooking spray and set aside.

FOR THE CAKE:

Whisk together flour, baking powder, and salt in a medium mixing bowl and set aside.

Mix together butter and sugar for about 1 minute. Add eggs, one at a time, and mix to thoroughly combine. Add vanilla and mix well. Add flour mixture to egg batter and mix until just combined. Transfer batter to the prepared pan and spread evenly. This will appear to be a very small amount of batter. Bake on the middle rack of oven 20 to 25 minutes, or until the cake is lightly golden.

Remove cake pan to a cooling rack and allow to cool 30 minutes. Poke the top of the cake all over with a skewer or fork. Allow the cake to cool completely and prepare the glaze.

FOR THE GLAZE:

Whisk together evaporated milk, sweetened condensed milk, and half-and-half in a bowl until combined. Pour glaze over the cake. Refrigerate the cake overnight.

FOR THE TOPPING:

Place cream, sugar, and vanilla into a medium bowl. Using a mixer on high speed, beat until stiff peaks are formed. Change to medium speed and whisk until thick. Spread topping over the cake and allow to chill in the refrigerator until ready to serve.

Makes 16 servings.

Spinach Lasagna Rolls

Garlic Breadsticks

Parmesan Spinach-Stuffed Mushrooms

Parmesan Spinach-Stuffed Mushrooms

These stuffed mushrooms are perfect for a party, appetizer, game night, or a side dish at dinner.

1½ cups hot water

1 (6-ounce) package stuffing mix for chicken

2 pounds fresh mushrooms (around 35)

2 tablespoons butter

2 cloves garlic, minced

1 cup chopped fresh spinach (or thawed frozen spinach)

1 cup shredded low-fat mozzarella cheese

1 cup grated Parmesan cheese

Preheat oven to 400 degrees F. Pour hot water over stuffing mix and stir until moistened. Cover and set aside. Remove stems from mushrooms and chop stems. Melt butter in a skillet over medium heat. Add chopped stems and garlic. Cook and stir for 5 minutes, or until tender, then add to the stuffing mixture, along with the spinach and cheeses. Mix well.

Spoon filling into the mushroom caps. Place them, filled-side up, on a baking sheet or in a shallow baking dish. Bake 20 minutes, or until mushrooms are tender and filling is heated through.

Makes about 20 stuffed mushrooms.

Spinach Lasagna Rolls

This meatless recipe pleases my whole family—even the carnivores. But you could easily add some meat to it if you want. —Elyse

10 ounces frozen chopped spinach, thawed and completely drained

15 ounces fat-free ricotta cheese

½ cup grated Parmesan cheese

1 egg

Salt, to taste

Freshly ground black pepper, to taste

1 (32-ounce) jar spaghetti sauce, divided

9 lasagna noodles, cooked

½ cup shredded part skim mozzarella cheese, or more, to taste

Preheat oven to 350 degrees F. Combine spinach, ricotta, Parmesan, egg, salt, and pepper in a medium bowl and set aside. Ladle about 1 cup spaghetti sauce onto the bottom of a 9x13-inch baking dish.

Lay out lasagna noodles on wax paper, making sure noodles are dry. Take ⅓ cup of ricotta mixture and spread evenly over noodle. Roll carefully and place seam-side down in the baking dish. Repeat with remaining noodles.

Ladle sauce over the noodles in the baking dish and top each one with shredded mozzarella cheese. Cover baking dish with foil and bake 40 minutes, or until cheese melts.

To serve, ladle a little sauce on the plate and top with lasagna roll.

Makes 9 rolls.

Garlic Breadsticks

When I lived in Salt Lake City, I loved going for a run early in the morning—not only to get exercise but also to smell all the bakeries cooking their delicious bread for the day. When I first tried these breadsticks, I fell in love instantly. —Kristen

18 frozen Rhodes Rolls	**Italian seasoning, to taste**
½ cup butter, melted	**Grated Parmesan cheese (optional)**
Garlic salt, to taste	

Thaw rolls until they are just a little cold. Roll dough balls into breadstick shapes (my girls call them snakes). Preheat oven to 350 degrees F.

Line up breadsticks up on a greased baking sheet so they are not touching each other (9 on each side of the pan)

Pour melted butter evenly over breadsticks. Cover with greased plastic wrap.

Let breadsticks rise until they are touching each other and the sides of the pan. Remove plastic wrap and sprinkle garlic salt, Italian seasoning, and Parmesan cheese, if using, over each breadstick.

Bake 20 minutes. Check on them after about 15 minutes. Bake until they are browned on top.

Makes 18 breadsticks.

MENU 46

Slow Cooker Sloppy Joes

Traditional American Macaroni Salad

No-Bake Lemon Icebox Cake

Slow Cooker Sloppy Joes

Want to know something hilarious? Six Sisters' Stuff has been approached by two different production companies about doing a reality TV show. Not even kidding. We have never once said that we are professional chefs; we are just trying to find the best and easiest recipes to keep our families fed. And these sloppy joes are seriously one of our family's favorites! I don't think it's fancy enough to be on any cooking show, but I guarantee that your family will love it. —Camille (P.S. We told both companies "no, thank you!")

1 pound ground turkey or ground beef	½ cup ketchup
1 onion, diced	2 tablespoons mustard
3 ribs celery, diced	1 tablespoon light brown sugar
1 green pepper, diced	Salt and pepper, to taste
1 (10.75-ounce) can condensed tomato soup	6 to 8 hamburger buns, toasted

In a large skillet, add ground meat, onion, celery, and green pepper, and cook over medium-high heat until meat is no longer pink. Place in slow cooker coated with cooking spray.

Add tomato soup, ketchup, mustard, and brown sugar to ingredients in slow cooker and stir together. Cook on low 4 hours; keep warm until serving. Serve on hamburger buns.

Makes 6 to 8 servings.

Traditional American Macaroni Salad

This is one of our favorite side dishes for a barbecue. It's creamy, full of flavor, and easy to make.

2 cups dry elbow macaroni, cooked, rinsed, and drained

⅓ cup diced celery

¼ cup minced red onion, soaked 5 minutes in cold water, drained

1 tablespoon minced flat-leaf parsley

½ cup diced vine-ripened tomato (optional)

½ cup mayonnaise

¾ teaspoon dry mustard

1½ teaspoons granulated sugar

1½ tablespoons cider vinegar

3 tablespoons sour cream

½ teaspoon kosher salt, plus more, to taste

Freshly ground black pepper

In a large bowl, combine macaroni, celery, onion, parsley, and tomato, if using. In a small bowl, whisk together mayonnaise, mustard, sugar, vinegar, sour cream, and salt. Pour dressing over salad and stir to combine. Season with salt and pepper, to taste. Serve.

Store covered in the refrigerator, for up to 3 days.

Makes 6 servings.

No-Bake Lemon Icebox Cake

I love those no-bake éclair cakes because of their simplicity and deliciousness. This cake was a winner with everyone who tried it. And it's even better the next day!

2 (3.5-ounce) packages instant lemon pudding mix

1 (8-ounce) container nondairy whipped topping

3 cups milk

1 (16-ounce) package graham crackers

LEMON FROSTING

½ cup butter, softened

1 to 2 cups powdered sugar

2 tablespoons milk

2 tablespoons lemon juice

In a large bowl, mix together pudding mixes, whipped topping, and milk.

Place a single layer of graham crackers on bottom of a 9x13-inch pan. (You may have to break a few graham crackers so that the entire bottom of the pan is covered). Spread half of pudding mixture evenly over graham crackers. Place another single layer of graham crackers on top of pudding and then layer the second half of pudding on top of crackers. Place one more single layer of graham crackers on top of pudding.

Mix together ingredients for lemon frosting and spread on top of cake. Cover and place in fridge about 4 hours.

Makes 12 servings.

MENU

47

Spinach and Artichoke Sandwich Melts

Fluffy Raspberry Jell-O Salad

Hershey's Cream Cheese Brownies

Fluffy Raspberry Jell-O Salad

Growing up, Sunday dinner just wasn't complete without a Jell-O salad. This is a great salad to make in the summer with fresh berries, and it makes a lot for a potluck dinner or a barbecue. If berries are not in season, it tastes just as good with frozen berries.

1   (4.6-ounce) package Jell-O Cook & Serve vanilla pudding (instant pudding will not work)

1   (6-ounce) package raspberry Jell-O

2   cups water

1   teaspoon lemon juice

1   (16-ounce) container nondairy whipped topping

2   cups raspberries, blackberries, or blueberries

Mix package contents of vanilla pudding and raspberry Jell-O with water and lemon juice in saucepan over medium heat, stirring constantly, until it boils. Remove from heat and pour into bowl. Refrigerate until mixture has thickened, about an hour. Beat until creamy. Fold in whipped topping and raspberries. Chill about an hour before serving.

Makes 10 servings.

Spinach and Artichoke Sandwich Melts

What could be better than your favorite dip slathered over some toasty bread? This recipe is a lighter version of traditional spinach and artichoke dip because it uses Greek yogurt and very little cream cheese. —Stephanie

1 tablespoon butter

1 teaspoon minced garlic

1 tablespoon all-purpose flour

½ cup milk

1 tablespoon cream cheese

½ cup shredded mozzarella cheese

½ cup grated Parmesan cheese

½ teaspoon black pepper

½ cup fat-free Greek yogurt

1 (6.7-ounce) jar grilled artichoke hearts, chopped

½ cup frozen chopped spinach, thawed and drained

1 loaf French bread, cut into 12 slices
    Butter, for spreading

Melt 1 tablespoon butter in a skillet over medium heat. Add minced garlic and cook 2 minutes. Whisk in flour until a paste forms. Cook over medium-low heat 1 minute, then pour in milk. Stir and cook 1 minute. If paste gets too thick, add a little milk to thin it out slightly. Add cream cheese, mozzarella, Parmesan, and pepper. Stir until cheeses are melted. Whisk in Greek yogurt until sauce is smooth. Fold in chopped artichokes and spinach.

Heat a skillet or griddle to medium-low heat. Butter one side of each slice of bread and spread 2 to 3 tablespoons of the cooked dip on the other side, with the buttered sides of bread on the outside. Cook sandwich until both sides of the bread are golden brown.

Makes 6 servings.

Hershey's Cream Cheese Brownies

I always stock up on chocolate bars because you never know when you might need them. The swirled cream cheese and the made-from-scratch brownies taste amazing together. —Kristen

10 tablespoons butter

3 ounces Hershey's milk chocolate chips

1 cup granulated sugar

2 large eggs

2 teaspoons vanilla extract

¾ cup all-purpose flour

¼ teaspoon salt

2 tablespoons unsweetened Hershey's cocoa powder

FOR THE CREAM CHEESE SWIRL

1 (8-ounce) package cream cheese, softened

⅓ cup granulated sugar

Pinch salt

1 large egg

2 teaspoons vanilla

5 (9.3-ounce) Hershey's chocolate bars

Preheat oven to 350 degrees F. Spray a 9x9-inch baking pan with cooking spray. In microwave, melt chocolate chips with butter, stirring every 30 seconds until smooth. Set aside. In a separate bowl, beat eggs and vanilla with sugar. Slowly add in chocolate mixture until well combined.

In small bowl, sift together cocoa, salt, and flour. Add dry mixture to egg batter and combine well. Pour batter into prepared baking pan.

For the cream cheese swirl, beat all ingredients together until smooth. Pour over brownie batter. Use sharp knife to swirl together.

Bake 50 to 60 minutes, or until just set and toothpick inserted comes out clean. Remove from oven and turn off heat. Top brownies with Hershey's bars and return to warm oven until melted enough to spread evenly over the surface. Allow to cool before cutting.

Makes 9 servings.

52
FAMILY DINNER CONVERSATION STARTERS

1. **What was the best** part of your day?

2. **If you could travel** anywhere in the world, where would you go and why?

3. **If you could be** a famous person for a week, who would you be and why?

4. **If you could have** any superpower, which would you choose?

5. **If you had one wish** (and no wishing for more wishes!), what would you wish for and why?

6. **If you could eat** just one food every day for a month and nothing else, what would it be?

7. **What is your** biggest fear?

8. **What is one way** you helped another person today?

9. **If you could trade** places with your parents for a day, what would you do differently?

10. **If you could have** one dream come true, what would it be?

11. **If you could pick** your own name, what would it be?

12. **If you could be** any animal, what would you be and why?

13. **Which character** in a book best describes you and why?

14. **If you could see** your future, where will you be in ten years?

15. **What are three** words that describe your sibling?

16. **If you could have** any pet, what would you choose and why?

17. **What is your favorite** childhood memory?

18. **What three words** would you use to describe yourself?

19. **What are the qualities** that make you a good friend?

20. **What is the nicest** thing a friend has ever done for you?

21. **What is your favorite** movie and why?

22. **What is your favorite** family tradition?

23. **What is your favorite** sport to play?

24. **If you could play** any instrument, what would it be and why?

25. **What is your favorite** holiday and why?

26. **What is one thing** you are grateful for today?

27. **What is your favorite** book and why?

28. **What has been** the happiest day of your life so far and why?

29. **What do you want** to be when you grow up and why?

30. **Where would you** like to go on our next family vacation?

31. **What is one thing** you could have done better today?

32. **Who is one person** in your life you are thankful for and why?

33. **What is the craziest** thing you've ever eaten?

34. **What is your earliest** memory?

35. **What is your most** embarrassing moment?

36. **What is your least** favorite chore?

37. **If you could only eat** three foods the rest of your life, which ones would they be?

38. **If you could have dinner** with anyone (past or present), who would it be and why?

39. **If you could stay up all night,** what would you do?

40. **What is the most** beautiful place you have ever seen?

41. **What is one thing** you couldn't live without?

42. **Who is your best** friend and why?

43. **If you had to live** in another country, which one would you choose?

44. **What is your greatest** talent or ability?

45. **What two items** would you grab if your house was on fire?

46. **If you could travel** back in time, when would you go?

47. **What is something** you want to learn how to do and why?

48. **What would you do** if you were a king or a queen?

49. **If you were invisible** for a day, what would you want to observe?

50. **If you had the attention** of the world for just ten seconds, what would you say?

51. **If you could give** your sibling an award, what would it be for?

52. **If you could be** a robot, a dinosaur, or a fairy, which one would you be and why?

Chicken Parmesan Crescents

Honey Cashew Green Beans

Chocolate Raspberry Brownie Parfaits

Chocolate Raspberry Brownie Parfaits

With only three ingredients, this dessert could not be any easier! I layer the brownies with the pudding and fresh raspberries in fancy goblets for the perfect summer dessert. —Camille

1   box brownie mix (or make your
    favorite homemade brownies)

1   (6-ounce) box chocolate instant
    pudding

2   cups fresh raspberries

Prepare brownies according to directions on box. Bake in a 9x13-inch pan as directed. Let cool completely. Once cooled, cut into small bite-size pieces. Prepare instant pudding as directed on box. Wash raspberries and pat dry. Layer brownies, pudding, and raspberries in glass or plastic cups.

Serve immediately.

Makes 8 servings.

Chicken Parmesan Crescents

My husband loves Chicken Parmesan, but it is a little too time-consuming to cook when I am trying to juggle two kids under the age of three. This recipe is so simple, even my picky three-year-old devoured it. —Camille

8 crispy chicken strips, fully cooked

1 (8-ounce) can refrigerated crescent rolls

8 slices mozzarella cheese

1 (24-ounce) jar spaghetti sauce

1 tablespoon butter, melted

¼ teaspoon garlic powder

½ teaspoon Italian seasoning

1 tablespoon grated Parmesan cheese

Cook chicken strips according to package directions. Preheat oven to 375 degrees F. Separate crescent rolls into 8 triangles. Place 1 slice of cheese on the wide end of each crescent roll. In a saucepan over low heat, warm spaghetti sauce until heated through. Dip cooked chicken strips in spaghetti sauce so they are completely covered.

Place dipped chicken strips on top of cheese and roll up crescent rolls. Place rolls on an ungreased baking sheet. Brush melted butter on top of each roll and sprinkle with mixture of garlic powder, Italian seasoning, and Parmesan cheese. Bake 15 minutes, or until golden brown.

Makes 8 servings.

Honey Cashew Green Beans

We love fresh green beans straight from the garden. Even my picky eaters will eat their vegetables when these beans are drizzled with this delicious glaze!

1	pound fresh or frozen green beans	½	cup cashews, coarsely chopped
3	tablespoons butter	2	tablespoons honey

Steam green beans until tender; drain and set aside in a saucepan. In a small skillet, sauté cashews in butter over low heat 5 minutes. Add honey and cook 1 minute longer, stirring constantly. Pour sauce over beans and toss until coated.

Makes 5 to 6 servings.

Slow Cooker Breakfast Casserole

Banana Crumb Muffins

Citrus Fruit Salad

Citrus Fruit Salad

This quick side dish is not only bright and colorful, but the added citrus flavor makes it amazing. On a hot summer day, it definitely hits the spot!

◇◇

1 cantaloupe, cut into bite-size pieces

1 pineapple, cut into bite-size pieces

1 pound strawberries, cut into bite-size pieces

¼ cup pulp-free orange juice

Pour all the fruit into a large bowl. Pour orange juice on top and mix well. Refrigerate until ready to serve. Mix again before serving.

Makes 6 servings.

Slow Cooker Breakfast Casserole

One of our favorite meals to have is breakfast for dinner (a.k.a. "brinner"). I prepped this recipe one morning and the kids absolutely devoured it for dinner. You could also easily make this the night before, put it in your slow cooker and let it cook 8 hours during the night, and wake up to an amazing breakfast. —Camille

1 (30-ounce) package frozen shredded hash brown potatoes

1 pound ground sausage, browned and drained

2 cups shredded cheddar cheese

½ cup shredded mozzarella cheese

1 onion, diced

1 green pepper, diced

1 red pepper, diced

12 eggs

½ cup milk

½ teaspoon salt

¼ teaspoon black pepper

Optional toppings: green onions, salsa, tomatoes, mushrooms, avocados

Spray a 6-quart slow cooker with nonstick cooking spray. (You cannot make this recipe in a smaller slow cooker because it won't fit.) Layer half of the potatoes on the bottom of slow cooker.

Top with half of the sausage, cheddar and mozzarella cheeses, onion, and green and red peppers. Repeat the layers again.

Beat eggs, milk, salt, and pepper in large bowl with a wire whisk until well blended. Pour egg mixture evenly over potato-sausage layers. Cook on low setting 8 hours or on high setting 4 hours, or until eggs are set. Top with green onions, salsa, tomatoes, mushrooms, avocado—whatever you like!

Makes 8 to 10 servings.

Banana Crumb Muffins

The crumb topping for this muffin is seriously divine! Mash some bananas and whip these up for a special person in your life. They will love you forever. —Camille

1½ cups all-purpose flour	3 bananas, mashed
1 teaspoon baking soda	¾ cup granulated sugar
1 teaspoon baking powder	1 egg, lightly beaten
½ teaspoon salt	⅓ cup butter, melted

CRUMB TOPPING

⅓ cup light brown sugar	⅛ teaspoon ground cinnamon
2 tablespoons all-purpose flour	1 tablespoon butter

Preheat oven to 375 degrees F. Place 16 muffin liners in muffin cups.

In a large bowl, mix together 1½ cups flour, baking soda, baking powder, and salt. In another bowl, beat together bananas, sugar, egg, and melted butter. Stir the banana mixture into the flour mixture until just moistened. Spoon batter into prepared muffin cups.

In a small bowl, mix together brown sugar, 2 tablespoons flour, and cinnamon. Cut in 1 tablespoon butter until mixture resembles coarse cornmeal. Sprinkle topping over muffins.

Bake 18 to 20 minutes, until a toothpick inserted into center of a muffin comes out clean.

Makes 16 muffins.

MENU 50

Cheeseburger Casserole

Honey Roasted Carrots

Caramel Oatmeal Cookies

Honey Roasted Carrots

One of the hardest things for me is making sure that I get in all my servings of vegetables every day. One of my friends suggested that I try her recipe for these honey roasted carrots, and I can seriously eat a whole pound of them in one sitting. —Camille

1	pound baby carrots	3	tablespoons honey
3	tablespoons olive oil		Salt and pepper, to taste

Preheat oven to 400 degrees F. Line a baking sheet with foil and spray lightly with cooking spray.

In a bowl, mix together carrots and olive oil until carrots are covered. Spread carrots in a single layer on a baking sheet. Drizzle honey over carrots and sprinkle salt and pepper on top. Bake uncovered, turning once, until just tender, about 25 to 30 minutes.

Makes 4 to 6 servings.

Cheeseburger Casserole

No bun needed to enjoy this fun take on a family favorite. Let's be honest—anything with pasta is delicious, but when you add the ingredients of a cheeseburger, the result is awesome.

2 cups (6 ounces) penne pasta	¾ teaspoon salt
2 teaspoons olive oil	½ teaspoon black pepper
1 onion, finely chopped	1 (28-ounce) can diced tomatoes
1 garlic clove, finely chopped	2 tablespoons Dijon mustard
1 pound lean ground beef (95 percent lean) or ground turkey	2 cups reduced-fat cheddar cheese, grated

Preheat the oven to 350 degrees F. Spray a 9x13-inch baking dish with cooking spray. In a large pot of boiling water, cook pasta according to the package directions. Drain well.

In a large skillet, heat oil over medium-low heat. Add onions and cook until soft, about 5 minutes. Stir in garlic and cook 30 seconds. Stir in beef and cook until browned; season with salt and pepper, to taste.

Add diced tomatoes and mustard; stir well. Let mixture simmer until slightly thickened, about 2 minutes. Season with salt and pepper.

Put noodles in greased pan and pour meat sauce on top. Slightly mix together noodles and sauce. Cover with foil and bake 20 minutes. Take it out of the oven and remove foil. Add cheese on top and return to the oven until the cheese is melted, 5 to 10 minutes.

Makes 8 servings.

Caramel Oatmeal Cookies

I love the chewy, soft texture of oatmeal cookies. I thought the only way to make them any better was to add bits of caramel. These may be my family's new favorite cookie! —Camille

1½ cups all-purpose flour

1 teaspoon baking soda

1 teaspoon cinnamon

1 teaspoon salt

1 cup butter, softened

¾ cup granulated sugar

¾ cup light brown sugar

2 eggs

1 teaspoon vanilla extract

3 cups quick or old-fashioned oats, uncooked

1 package Kraft Caramel Bits

Preheat oven to 350 degrees F. In a small bowl, combine flour, baking soda, cinnamon, and salt.

In a large bowl, cream together butter, granulated sugar, brown sugar, eggs, and vanilla extract. Gradually beat in flour mixture.

Fold in oats and caramel bits. Drop by rounded tablespoons onto baking sheets lined with parchment paper.

Bake 10 to 12 minutes, or until golden brown.

Makes 5 dozen cookies.

MENU 51

Buffalo Chicken Salad Sandwiches

Mom's Potato Salad

Cheesecake Chess Squares

Cheesecake Chess Squares

I had a ton of cream cheese in my fridge when I came across these Cheesecake Chess Squares. They seemed too simple, but thought I would give them a try. Holy Cow! My husband doesn't eat very many treats but he came home for lunch just to grab a couple of these. *Delicious* is all I can say! —Kristen

1 (18.25-ounce) box yellow cake mix	4 cups powdered sugar
½ cup butter, melted	1 (8-ounce) package cream cheese, softened
3 eggs, divided	

Preheat oven to 300 degrees F. Spray a 9×13-inch dish with cooking spray.

Mix cake mix, melted butter, and 1 egg into a soft dough. Press into the bottom of the pan. Mix the powdered sugar, cream cheese, and remaining 2 eggs until smooth. Pour on top of crust and bake 40 to 50 minutes, until top is golden brown.

Makes 12 servings.

Buffalo Chicken Salad Sandwiches

If you are looking for a quick and easy dinner, look no further. These sandwiches are perfect for hot summer days because you don't even have to turn your oven on. My family absolutely loves them. —Camille

2 cups cooked and shredded chicken (I used a rotisserie chicken)

½ cup ranch dressing

¼ cup hot buffalo wing sauce (I like Frank's RedHot sauce)

4 ounces cream cheese, softened

2 ribs celery, finely diced

¼ cup finely diced onion

¼ teaspoon garlic powder

Salt and pepper, to taste

Buns

Optional toppings: tomatoes, cheese, lettuce, pickles

In a large bowl, mix together chicken, ranch dressing, buffalo sauce, cream cheese, celery, onion, and garlic powder. Add salt and pepper as needed.

Serve on buns and top with your favorite sandwich fixings.

Store leftovers in a covered container in the fridge.

Makes 4 to 6 servings.

Mom's Potato Salad

Mom's Potato Salad is so delicious and it brings back so many memories of growing up, not to mention it is the easiest potato salad recipe I have ever made! —Kristen

8 potatoes, cooked and diced into bite-size pieces

8 eggs, hard boiled

¾ cup dill or sweet pickles, diced

2 ribs celery, diced

1 cup mayonnaise

2 to 3 tablespoons yellow mustard

1 tablespoon granulated sugar

1 teaspoon white vinegar

Salt and pepper, to taste

Salad Supreme seasoning, optional

Boil eggs 15 minutes. Drain and rinse boiled eggs under cold water. Put in fridge to cool.

Once cool, combine potatoes, celery, and pickles in a large bowl. Dice eggs and add to the bowl.

To make the sauce, combine in a separate bowl mayonnaise, mustard, sugar, and vinegar. Pour sauce over the potato mixture and combine. Add salt and pepper, to taste. If salad is dry, add more mayonnaise to get the texture you like.

Top with Salad Supreme. You may also save 1 hardboiled egg to slice for garnishing on top.

Makes 10 servings.

MENU 52

Low-Fat Turkey Bacon Wrap

Sweet Spaghetti Squash

S'mores Kiss Cookies

Low-Fat Turkey Bacon Wrap

I was getting really sick of my usual salad for lunch so I've been switching things up. This low-fat turkey bacon wrap is delicious! —Kristen

2	tablespoons fat-free ranch dressing	3	pieces turkey bacon
1	multigrain wrap		Sliced tomato
2	slices of deli turkey		Romaine lettuce

Spread the ranch dressing on the inside of the multigrain wrap. Add the rest of the ingredients as desired and roll up the wrap. Cut in half for easier eating.

Makes 1 serving.

Sweet Spaghetti Squash

This is one squash recipe your whole family will eat. Perhaps the brown sugar and butter have a little to do with that, but at least there is some squash in there too!

1 medium spaghetti squash

6 tablespoons butter

¼ cup light brown sugar

½ tablespoon ground cinnamon

½ cup chopped pecans

Salt and pepper, to taste

Preheat oven to 350 degrees F. Cut squash in half lengthwise. Scoop out the seeds then place the halves cut-side down in a baking dish filled with enough water to cover the bottom of the dish. Bake 1 hour, or until the shell of the squash is flexible and the inside is tender. Let squash cool 10 to 15 minutes. Using a fork, scrape out the inside of the squash to form strands. Place all of the squash strands into a large bowl and toss with butter, brown sugar, cinnamon, pecans, salt, and pepper. Serve hot.

Makes 8 servings.

S'mores Kiss Cookies

These cookies are just like eating s'mores, only without the smoke-scented clothing at the end of the night.
—Elyse

1   cup graham cracker crumbs

1¼ cups all-purpose flour

½   teaspoon baking soda

½   teaspoon salt

½   cup unsalted butter, room temperature

½   cup light brown sugar

⅓   cup granulated sugar

1   large egg

1   teaspoon vanilla extract

20 large marshmallows, cut in half

About 40 chocolate kisses

Preheat oven to 350 degrees F. In a large bowl, combine graham cracker crumbs, flour, baking soda, and salt. Set aside.

In another bowl, beat butter and sugars together until creamy and smooth. Add in egg and vanilla extract and mix until combined.

Slowly add the dry ingredients and mix until just combined. Drop rounded tablespoons of dough onto a baking sheet, 1 to 2 inches apart.

Bake 6 to 8 minutes or until edges are just golden brown. Remove from oven and gently press half a marshmallow, sticky side down, onto each cookie. Let cool completely.

Once cookies are cooled, preheat broiler. Place cookies back on baking sheets and broil 1 to 2 minutes, keeping a close eye on them so they don't burn. Once marshmallows are golden brown, remove from the broiler and place a chocolate kiss on top of each cookie.

Makes approximately 3 dozen cookies.

BIRTHDAY BANNER/CHAIR

When we were small, my mom always made our birthdays special. Now that I have kids, I love making their birthdays special. One thing we do in our family is a Birthday Chair.

I have the chair all decorated so when the birthday child wakes up, he or she can eat breakfast in it along with all the other meals. —Kristen

WHAT YOU'LL NEED

- 5 pieces of 8½x11-inch felt (I used 2 hot pink, 2 silver, and 1 white)
- Black permanent marker
- String or ribbon
- Glue gun or glue dots
- Scissors

INSTRUCTIONS

1. **Cut out** thirteen triangles from the felt. Each triangle should measure 5x5x3 each. (I cut seven in hot pink and six in silver). You will use these to spell out the words "Happy Birthday."

5. **Thread a ribbon** or string through the holes punched into the triangles.

6. **Tie the banner** onto the chair. Be creative. And don't forget the balloons!

2. **Punch two holes** on the short side of each triangle.

3. **Write the letters** with permanent marker on a contrasting felt color and cut them out.

4. **If you choose** to print out the letters from your computer, make sure they will fit onto your triangles. Using a glue gun or glue dots, glue your letters onto your triangles.

INDEX